A LIFE OF SONG

A LIFE OF SONG

Robert Yates

Published by Robert Yates in collaboration with
The Larks Press
Ordnance Farmhouse
Guist Bottom
Dereham NR20 5PF
01328 829207

June, 2002

Printed by the Lanceni Press,
Garrood Drive, Fakenham

British Library Cataloguing-in-Publication Data
A catalogue record for this book is available from the British Library.

Acknowledgment

Finding myself totally inept at composing this document by means of a typewriter or word processor, I am indebted to Josie Bramley for so diligently deciphering my appalling scrawl, and with her typing expertise enabling these memoirs to be produced. R.Y.

© Robert Yates – 2002

ISBN 1 904006 05 1

Preface

I commenced writing these memoirs with a view to providing a family record of my singing experience, linked with those of my wife, Audrey.

It became apparent that the early years of music making had to be autobiographical. I became bored with this, and the project was abandoned for many years. My interest was re-kindled when I decided to sort out the programmes and press critiques that we had accumulated, and which had never received more attention than being thrown into a cardboard box.

The result of this activity is depicted in the following pages by a yearly listing of performances to which we contributed, accompanied by such anecdotes as the memory has retained.

Robert Yates

The Yates Family c.1918,
the author on his mother's knee

Foreword

Bob, to an impressionable schoolgirl in the fifties, was a local equivalent of the current film star idol Gregory Peck - dashing, handsome and protective, yet utterly safe and dependable. I was first aware of him, as Lord Mountararat in a production of *Iolanthe* at the Theatre Royal in the mid-fifties - his noble stature and rich, forthright rendition of 'When Britain really ruled the waves' won my heart, and I never dreamed that I would play alongside him in the near future in *The Beggar's Opera* (I was one of the 'Ladies of the Town', with only the haziest notion of what that meant) and *Mr Pepys*, (first in a succession of demurely innocent 'mob-cap' roles, and also, significantly my first experience of performing in front of a work's composer). Later on, we appeared together in Sidney Twemlow's little opera group, during the time I taught at Aylsham School, and was directly responsible to him as County Music Advisor.

At a formative time in my life. Bob and Audrey (how can one separate them? - as a team they are inimitable) provided, in addition to their formidable vocal and thespian skills, an ideal example of commitment, charisma, enterprise, zest for life, and youthfulness of spirit - all on-going as of now. It was a privilege, and a marvellous training, to sing beside them as I took the first steps towards a professional career.

In later years, Bob's incredible energy and imagination was devoted to the activities of the Norfolk Opera Players, yet he still found time for special projects, most notably the sterling achievement of the staged *Elijah* in the Cathedral - a cherished ambition, triumphantly realised. Today's world of large budgets, funding problems and the complicated logistics of theatre production, inevitably mean that involvement even at an 'amateur' level in a theatrical enterprise is a huge and time-consuming challenge. Happily, the NOP continues to function and enrich the musical life of Norwich, and Bob's role in its history can never be under-estimated. His comic verses describing each production are an added delight ...is there no limit to his talents?

On a personal level, we've remained in touch over the years, and the loyalty and generosity that Bob and Audrey have always shown to me and my husband Tony Payne is a great boon. Bob's characteristically well-judged and witty speech at our wedding is vivid amongst many memories, and we've enjoyed countless social occasions together.

Live music-making has to remain as the central plank of musical experience, whether amateur or professional, or something in-between. It's sad to reflect oft the enormous changes wrought by the influence of the media in encouraging passivity and vicarious enjoyment, and the impatient quest for instant gratification, as a substitute for active and lovingly-prepared participation.

This memoir chronicles an artistic life of rich variety and unassailably high principles wedded to a grasp of practicalities, against a back-drop of a changing world. It will stir up many memories, both recent and distant. It also charts the

5

developing framework of the performing arts in the rural community, and their nurture, often requiring iron resolve and fortitude. The Yates's have played a towering and vital role in this journey, and they deserve our gratitude.

Jane Manning. 2002

Chapter 1

'Since singing is so good a thing
I wish all men would learn to sing'.

William Byrd's entreaty, though not encountered in my beginnings, would have needed no publicity in my household, since from an early age I was possessed of a compulsion to sing.

My earliest experience however established me as a critic rather than as an exponent, for I developed a dislike of the fervent tenor voice of a member of the small choir of the primitive Methodist Church at the bottom of our lane. Since then, I have referred to any perpetrator of such a vocal assault as a 'chapel tenor'. It is not greatly to my credit however that, to avoid this vocal violation, I frequently feigned sickness in order to escape and be taken home, where I would be questioned on what I had eaten for breakfast. I do recall that the outcome of these enquiries apportioned blame equally and variously to bacon and egg, porridge and kipper. Embarrassingly, it was sometimes the 'chapel tenor' himself who took me home! He was quite a nice man.

Release from all this came at the age of eight, when my brother and sister (who were twins) and I moved from Postwick school to Thorpe school. At morning hymn singing the headmaster, in company with the choirmaster of Thorpe church, passed up and down our serried ranks, and apparently heard in me sufficient promise to invite me to join the church choir. My brother was also invited, not because of any outstanding vocal talent (he had other attributes), but in order to keep me company. After all, we lived two miles from the church, and a mile from the nearest bus stop, and joining the choir would involve two choir practices a week and three services on Sundays.

My parents were pleased, and my achievement inspired mother to induce me to sing to her piano accompaniments, which were strictly basic, executed on a wooden-framed piano which doubtless had not recently if ever received the ministrations of a piano tuner. In permanent residence on the top was a porcelain bust of Gluck (which I have now). I think my sister Norah also struggled to accompany. The only tune I can remember from these episodes is 'Peggy O'Neil'.

There was an initiation ceremony for new recruits to the choir, performed by established choir boys, which consisted of being slung into the yew bush, this bush being situated just inside the church gate. I think we survived this ceremony without too much trauma, although the bush concealed a gravestone which had been known to leave its mark on one or two of the less fortunate.

My introduction to the church ritual and hymn singing was one of the most exciting experiences of my life. It is difficult to express the exhilaration and intoxication that pervaded my unfledged soul. Even now I can experience this euphoria upon hearing any of the hymns that we sang in the earliest of those days. The ritual too, at that time, must have aroused the emotions. There were purple cassocks and white surplices for the choir, and red cassocks for the servers; there were processions around the church on festival Sundays, always attracting a full congregation, and sometimes with contingents of uniformed organisations, attending for the church blessing on some milestone in their careers.

All of this was so different from the unpretentious chapel service with its unappealing tenor, and, to me it's unattractive hymns. Not that the 'chapel tenor' syndrome was entirely absent from the Thorpe choir, but with a muster of about sixteen men, it was somewhat muted. Moreover, in later years the daughter of the Thorpe 'chapel tenor' was the subject of my secret infatuation, and covert glances from my choir stall to her pew were too frequent to be discreet. Alas, I never had occasion to speak to her, because she and her mother had always ensconced themselves in the family car by the time I had emerged from the vestry, ready to be driven off by the father and two sons (both also choir members, of whom more anon). Anyway, I think part of me wanted to retain the mystery of dark eyes and pale complexion embraced in the warmth of winter furs. Perhaps also I would have been too shy to have uttered a word anyway (there was no co-education in those days and girls were fairly remote beings except for those in one's immediate circle). I might also have had regard for the adage 'Before you marry the daughter, look well on the mother'. Well, the mother didn't look up to much.

I do not wish to denigrate my brother's singing ability; in fact, he was quite as good as some of the other boys, but he wasn't solo material, whereas I had been honoured with the belief that I was. This confidence in me (and by me) was to be exhibited later on by the choirmaster asking me to sing the solo part in an anthem entitled 'Come Holy Ghost, Our Souls Inspire', but because it would have been my first solo, Allan was deputed to sing it with me. It went quite well as far as I can remember. I suppose I must have been about twelve and Allan about fourteen. His voice must have broken after that, for he became a server for a short time, then left and found another interest in the Priory Gymnasium.

At this time in our lives, and in the summer months, we all swam in the river at Postwick Grove, polluted even then, but disregarded by us all in spite of one boy who swam upstream at Whitlingham Reach contracting typhoid fever and dying from it. In the summer, in spite of my love of river swimming, such was my enthusiasm for the choir that I would abbreviate my stay at the Grove and run all the way to church (two miles) for choir practice on Tuesdays and Fridays.

The adult members of the choir were a mixed bag, but had one common characteristic – they were all male. The schoolmaster who introduced me was a useful bass. Another man had a deep basso profundo voice (probably derived from smoking or from bronchial tendencies), whose main contribution to the harmony was in the nether regions, which he supported with considerable gusto. Bronchial or not, I saw him in later years when he must have been a great age, still pedalling a bicycle more ancient than himself.

Another bass was looked upon (by me at least) as a 'gentleman', because he lived in a big house. In fact I think he was fully deserving of that title, for I have nothing but pleasant recollections of his actions and comportment. As far as singing was concerned he sang a fairly inoffensive bass, which perhaps gave a softer edge to the stentorian tones of the man with the bicycle. (Another point in his favour was that he gave me a record of Ernest Lough singing 'I know that my Redeemer liveth' after I had sung it in church. (Not that I was destined to hear it too many times – my brother sat on it).

One of the other singers had a bass voice, but instead of singing the bass part, he sang the melody an octave down. I cannot recall whether the choirmaster ever remonstrated with him on this matter, but his wife was an indefatigable church worker, so perhaps politics were involved.

A tenor ('chapel' by definition) took the number one position in the choir stalls. His higher ululations were in competition with the lower declamations of the aforementioned cyclist. Two of his sons (brothers of the object of my secret adulation referred to earlier) also sang tenor, one reasonably, the other negligibly.

Another tenor had a son who had the reputation of being a bully, and I recall an historic fight in which he was bested by a weight-lifting friend of my brother. No evidence of bullying came from the bully's dad, who sang a very good tenor, and seemed a rational enough man.

In addition to all of these, and others of whom my memory is less sharp, the choir included a male alto, a goldsmith by profession, who had such over-whelming desire to be heard that he always hung on to concluding notes longer than anyone else. I came near to hating that man.

Curiously, I have a somewhat fainter memory of most of the boys, perhaps because they were a transient element. There were always about sixteen of us, a number that I think would be hard to muster in most village choirs today. Thorpe was a compact village then, and everybody knew everybody else. Perhaps the attraction of choir singing then was the reward of 'tuppence' on Sunday, and half-a-crown a quarter, with the expectation of other half-crowns at weddings and funerals. Moreover, there was no television then, and records were played on wind-up gramophones.

I do remember the head boy and soloist at the time of my joining. He did everything a head boy should do, including looking after the new recruits. In later years I was to become best man at his wedding, and he at mine. I remember also his successor, a most attractive boy with an extremely beautiful voice, and possessing a talent for sport. Unfortunately his sporting talent extended to a productive meeting with a willing member of the opposite sex, precipitating his banishment to the navy at the age of fourteen.

In my turn, I enjoyed a good run as Head Boy and as boy soloist, with singing assignments including 'Hear My Prayer', 'Oh, for the Wings of a Dove', 'I know that my Redeemer liveth', 'How beautiful are the feet'. In those days it was not possible to record such performances, so I cannot say how well or how badly I sang. I still thrill when I hear the introduction to 'I know that my Redeemer liveth', and do remember that I accomplished the breathing required in the long phrases.

My parents would come along to hear my solo efforts, my father I think reluctantly, for although he was very musical (trombone and 'cello) and applauded my vocal efforts, I formed the impression then, to be confirmed later, that his agnosticism was in conflict with the church ritual.

We were no different from boys of today, for whilst presumably assuming angelic mien in church, we were pretty uncouth outside, amongst other things invoking the wrath of the local shopkeeper by making such facetious requests as 'a ha'peth of sticky sweets please'. A chase would sometimes ensue, much to our gratification. On occasions we would buy five Woodbines for 'tuppence' to smoke surreptitiously en route to choir practice. We had to be on the alert for the village policeman who patrolled regularly by bicycle in those days, by carefully concealing cigarette in cupped hand in pocket when he passed.

I think my voice broke when I was fourteen. I resisted the request of the choirmaster to carry on and sing alto while the voice was settling. This decision was not an easy one to take, since I was indebted to the choirmaster (Arthur Daniels) who had promoted me on every possible occasion, and with whom I practised new pieces regularly after choir practice. However, opinions I had heard expressed led me to believe that to continue singing at this stage might damage the voice. Right or wrong, I have never regretted making that decision. Instead, I agreed to become a server until my adult voice developed. I never enjoyed this role, which was purely ritualistic, and during this period I skipped services whenever I could.

When my new voice arrived it wasn't deep enough to sing bass, since the bass parts in hymns are generally fairly low in the stave, so for a time I sang a very indifferent and limited tenor. Later on, as a bass, still in my teens, I was asked to sing the bass solos in Stainer's 'Crucifixion', and decided to take singing lessons with William Hunn, then a leading figure on the Yarmouth musical scene. He taught amongst the pianos on the first floor of Howlett's piano shop in Norwich then situated opposite Jarrolds, now a Burton's establishment. I marvel to think that in those days I took such songs and arias along to him as 'To the Forest' (Tchaikowsky) and 'Largo al Factotum' (Rossini). I must have been precocious. On the other hand, Mr Hunn himself brought along some very advanced songs for me to sing. In my new role as bass soloist, I received the same support from Mr Daniels as I had received before my voice broke, so that I was frequently called upon to sing a solo.

At this period of my life I had become a dance band drummer, purchasing the kit from my early wage packets, and practising in the wash-house at our second home in Norfolk Cottages, Yarmouth Road, Thorpe. My study was based on an instructional tutor by Max Abrahams, then the drummer with Ambrose and his Orchestra. I practised flans, paradiddles, five and nine stroke rolls, and the Joe Daniels' 'breaks' relentlessly, and bashed away for hours accompanying records of Nat Gonella, Lionel Hampton, Tommy Dorsey et al. Amazingly I cannot recall that there were ever any complaints from neighbours. They must have been more generous than I am now, because the sound of someone's transistor radio penetrating my domain sends me berserk.

My first dance band experience was with 'Mac and his Manhattans' playing at the Margaret Harker Hall, Blofield. It was Mac's band, and he had recruited my father on trombone, Harry Aldred trumpet, Fred Cheshire guitar, Jack Ramshaw piano, and himself violin. In addition to the tunes of the day we were called upon to play tunes written by Mac himself. I think our attitude to these pieces was one of humouring him, because he was the boss. I suppose they were well written, but in a country dance hall, then, as now, dancers expected to hear the popular tunes of the day. Publishers were always pushing new tunes, of course, and if broadcasting bands could be persuaded to play them, they could become popular by repetition. Some, of course were absolute junk, and I drew the line at singing 'When Charlie did his courting in a Chalk Pit'.

A special bus would pick us up with all our accoutrements, our regular followers, mostly from Norwich, having already installed themselves. They were very bright occasions, but we never made any money there. I have an old balance sheet somewhere showing a profit carried forward of 2s. 7½d. Our earliest days there were before the advent of the microphone, and Dad, Fred Cheshire and I would sing three-part harmonies arranged by Dad, through cardboard megaphones made by him and painted gold. One of these arrangements was 'The Broadway Melody'; another was 'Black Coffee'. There were others.

Our Blofield days must have stretched over several years, because it was two house-moves onwards that I encountered Russell Mason, our next-door neighbour's son, who was technically minded and had developed an amplification system. The speaker was about four feet square and just liftable by two people. This is the apparatus that superseded the megaphones at Blofield, and precipitated a new challenge for the bus conductor who previously had only to wrestle with my drum kit and dad's trombone. I think I can remember the more-than-occasional feed-back from that apparatus. Anyway, I was personally indebted to Russell for other reasons. It was he who introduced me to music that I had hitherto not known. He had installed a gramophone in his shed, and there we listened to Tchaikowsky's 'Andante Cantabile', the overture to *'Lohengrin'*, Laurence Tibbet singing 'Largo al Factotum' and many other vocal gems, which must have been an inspiration to me.

He had also devised a system of recording on aluminium discs, and in the sanctity of that outbuilding, I recorded 'Is it true what they say about Dixie?' I wish I knew what happened to that disc – I know that I treasured it.

Others whose bands I played with before the war were Eddie Gates, Billy Beales, The Norwich Accordion Band, Bert Priest, Bert Galey, and the Norwich Municipal Dance Orchestra, at venues including village halls, holiday camps, hotels, Chapelfield Gardens, Little Plumstead Hall, and I suppose the most prestigious, the Lido (later to become The Norwood Rooms, and now, alas, a Bingo Hall).

A memory, which I have of those days, is of the odd occasions that Bert Galey, the pianist and I would go back-stage at the Hippodrome (long demolished) to take stock of the acts, which on the Saturday evening would come to the Lido after their performance to give a floor show. We would be required to provide some background music. On one occasion I witnessed a striptease act at very close quarters, whilst chatting to another scantily-clad girl in the wings. I must confess that the proximity of the latter warmed me more than the sight of the former. The utmost decorum was displayed back-stage, as the nude lady was immediately draped by a colleague.

Cars were few in those days, and apart from engagements at Holiday Camps, or places deep into the county, one travelled by public transport, bicycle or on foot. My kit, consisting of bass drum, snare drum and a case containing cymbals, foot cymbals, snare drum stand, trap tray, temple blocks, cow bells, foot pedal, sticks and brushes would all have to go under the stairs on the bus. I can't imagine anyone suffering this in these days. On one occasion I remember carrying all this equipment six miles from Earlham Fiveways to Thorpe at about one o'clock in the morning, with the bass drum under my left arm, and the snare drum carried outside that, and the case of ironmongery in the right hand. (I often wondered why I had not taken up the flute). On some of these occasions I sang with the band, which meant that I could be singing 'Dark Town Strutter's Ball' on Saturday, and 'The Trumpet shall Sound' on Sunday.

Chapelfield Garden dances were held every Monday in the summer, in the mid or late thirties, admission eightpence. The concrete area around the bandstand would be liberally strewn with French chalk. They were quite spectacular occasions. The Municipal Dance Orchestra to which I had been recruited was comprised of members of the Municipal Orchestra who gave Saturday night concerts in St. Andrew's Hall. I was very flattered to have been asked, but their accomplishments as a dance band were not too great, though they were thoroughly good musicians. Anyway, I sang such songs as 'In the Still of the Night', 'The Night is Young and You're so Beautiful', 'Begin the Beguine', and many others.

The fee for an evening's dance band work, playing from 8–12 midnight would normally be ten shillings. An 8 p.m.–1.00 a.m. stint would fetch fifteen shillings, and on festival days such as Boxing Day, one would be paid £1. These sums, sounding ridiculous today, were a fair augmentation of my commencing salary at the age of sixteen of £40 per annum, rising by 1940, I think, to about £120 per annum.

These pre-war dance band days were memorable chiefly for my love of rhythm, and for the tunes, the best of which are still being played today. Socially, those days were not significantly memorable, because we were doing a job of work, enabling others to socialise. An exception to this was a series of engagements with Eddie Gates and his band at Drayton Village Hall. Eddie was blind, but played piano and piano accordion quite miraculously. During this period I suppose my drum kit must have stayed at Drayton Village Hall, because I would cycle from my home at Thorpe to the County Council offices (then encompassing Nos. 23-31 Thorpe Road), leave my bicycle there, and join a coach at Thorpe Station, especially commissioned to take the band and the dancers (we had regular camp-followers). Eddie would be accompanied by his father Charles Gates who was in business as an electrical engineer, with premises near Foundry Bridge.

This is where the social bit comes in. I was at that time courting a girl called Jessie who lived at Framingham Earl. On arriving back in Norwich from Drayton, Charles Gates would quite frequently expect Jessie and me to go to his premises to play cards with him and Eddie. We played with Braille-marked cards, and I think the game must have been Solo. This of course would take us to the early hours of Sunday morning. In due course Jessie and I would walk up the hill to the Council Offices, where she also had left her bicycle. My bike was usually ill-equipped for night riding. Now, in those days there were always several cycles left in the cycle racks over the week-end, and I would borrow one better equipped than mine, and return it early on Monday morning, an action not morally sustainable perhaps, but never harmful. You will have to believe that cycles could be left without fear of theft in those days. Then Jessie and I would cycle to Framingham Earl where she would invite me in to eat a cold meat supper, her parents having retired to bed somewhat earlier. Her father was a cattle dealer, and there was always a choice of about three different joints (all prime cuts). In those days I had a voracious appetite, and relished these occasions. I would then cycle home to Thorpe and turn in about 3.00 a.m, returning the borrowed cycle to the County Council cycle shed before 9.00 a.m. on the Monday morning.

On one of these occasions, we were hailed to stop by a policeman on foot duty. Feeling confident that my bicycle was properly equipped, we dismounted, only for me to discover that Jessie's bike had no white flap (legally required to be affixed to the rear mudguard in those days). I have to admit that I ordered Jessie to remount. We both pedalled madly to outpace the running policeman, and Jessie's heartbeat did not return to normal until we reached Framingham Earl.

This appears to be the correct moment to admit to a similar incident which developed from my losing my cycle lamp at the Fox and Hounds, Little Plumstead where, together with other staff of the Architect's Department, I had been regaling the locals with songs to my ukulele accompaniment. On the way home, I was protected by two other cyclists who rode one either side of me. Unfortunately this did not deceive the local bobby travelling in the other direction; he promptly turned tail and pursued. I decided to go it alone, and won the race in sufficient time to take my cycle indoors, through the house and out the back, telling my father what had happened and asking him to say that I was not at home. Reluctantly he perjured himself, but the constable was not deceived, and the next morning he was on the doorstep, giving me a severe warning, but forbearing to put me behind bars or even to extract a fine, speaking volumes I think for the empathy that the village policeman enjoyed with the public in those days. There were other incidents when policemen gave chase (unsuccessfully), because of our failure to ensure that we were properly equipped with lights and white flap.

I think that this is the time to mention another musical activity, which occupied me in these pre-war days. We had moved house, and found ourselves living next door to a young couple, Ralph and Babs Potter. He was a pianist, and she a singer. They were members of a concert party called The Harmonics. For any young reader of this document, I would explain that this form of entertainment took place in village halls, country houses, theatres large and small, and consisted of two essential ingredients, a compère and a pianist, and variously of a comedian, singers male and female, sometimes including a soubrette. With The Harmonics, Babs took this latter role and Ralph was both pianist and compère. All performances were made, whether in large or small halls, without the aid of microphones and attendant equipment. These neighbours, learning of my singing proclivities, persuaded me to join their concert party as a 'straight' singer.

The first concert to which I contributed was in a barn at Strumpshaw. The audience was variously disposed on chairs, bales of hay, and roof rafters. An ice-cream lady was pedalling her wares, and an air of bonhomie prevailed. The stage was made of long planks set on boxes. The entire company sang the opening chorus. Does my memory serve me wrongly when I recollect that we were dressed as Russian pierrots? My turn came. Ralph, as compère said: 'Ladies and gentlemen, we now present Robert Yates, up-and-coming baritone from Norwich. He will sing for you "I Travel the Road"'. I mounted the stage, suitably dressed in a sort of khaki ensemble, complete with slouch hat - and went straight through the stage! I remember Ralph making puns to the audience whilst the stage was being repaired, such as: 'I hope you're not too board.' Anyway, I think the song must have gone all right at the second attempt, because I cannot recall further calamity.

Later on, one of our commissions was to entertain at a large country house party. A lot of important people were there, and every room, including toilets, seemed to be lined with bottles of various alcoholic drinks, some opened, some unopened, with a view no doubt to sustaining the party spirit, whenever incidental activity drew people away from the house's social centre, and the site of our performance.

Among the guests was the grandson of William Holman Hunt, British artist most famous for his painting of 'The Light of the World'. He had obviously contributed substantially to the party spirit, but with great determination, and some difficulty, conducted us on a tour of the house. He was particularly anxious to show us a rather splendid wooden chair, of which he declared, more than once: 'There 'sh not a nail in't,' his final iteration being more liquescent than the first.

Before proceeding further, I would remark that this documentary concerns itself with musical activities and related experiences and impressions. It accordingly gives scant mention of family and friends, or activities such as sport and romances, all of which were included in a full life, outside my regular employment as a junior clerk, rising ultimately to executive status in the employ of the Norfolk County Council and the National Health Service.

Since this is not an autobiography but restricted to musical memories, it does relieve me conveniently of the necessity to tell all, to commit to paper all those memories which one prefers to forget, as well as those which would be of little interest to the reader, however well scripted.

However, I cannot omit one happening, which occurred just after the outbreak of war. My brother was killed when riding his motorcycle. This was a devastating blow to us all, as a result of which I did not immediately volunteer for war service, but waited until conscripted in June 1940. I will try to restrict my wartime experiences to those, which had musical connotations, but inevitably some supporting material will be necessary.

During early training days at Kempston Barracks, Bedford, as a rookie with the Beds. & Herts. Light Infantry, I was able to hear the BBC strings conducted by Sir Adrian Boult, in Bedford Corn Hall. Later I was to be transferred to the military police.

Like many men, my six years of war service had its ups and downs. One of its 'downs' was to contract diphtheria and walk about with it for two months before being diagnosed. I will try to be brief. Admitted to hospital in Carlentini (Sicily) and diagnosed as having Vincent's Angina, I spent eleven days quite comfortably before discharge. During these eleven days my unit had moved to Italy. I hitch-hiked along the coast to Riposto in the back of a truck, and went for a swim in the sea to cleanse myself of dust. I nearly didn't get back, for my heart started beating at about 100 mph. Surviving this, I hitch-hiked over to Italy on an L.C.T. (Landing Craft Tanks), spent a week billeted in the cells at Taranto jail (the only accommodation available), bitten whilst there by mosquitoes and bugs, travelled up the Adriatic coast in search of my unit, eventually finding them at Trani. Whilst there I began to lose feeling in the tips of my fingers and toes.

In a worsening condition, I had to return to Sicily as prosecuting witness in a manslaughter charge, and surviving this (just), I was diagnosed as having had diphtheria, was admitted to hospital in Catania, later moved back to Tunis, then to Algiers (variously in diphtheria and polio wards). Following complete paralysis, I miraculously turned the scale in Algiers (where my service abroad had started) in response to electrical massage, and from there proceeded to the convalescent depot in Sidi Feruche near Algiers.

Upon arrival I still had very little voice and certainly no singing voice, which I thought had gone forever. One day, after about three months' convalescence, amazingly it returned, and I joined the camp Choral Society and the Concert Party. In the choral society I was asked to sing the bass solos in some sea shanties. A B.B.C. representative of the Forces Expeditionary Station at Algiers was present in the audience, and I must have sung pretty well, because he invited me to sing solos from the radio station. The camp padre provided me with songs, which he mysteriously produced from somewhere. They included 'Harlequin' (by Wilfred Sanderson) with a bottom E flat, which I accomplished quite well, I think, possibly assisted by the pint of beer and a raw Spanish onion which I discovered were good 'looseners'. Then there was 'The Blind Ploughman' (a bit of Victorian sentimentality, but easy on the voice), a setting of R. L. Stevenson's 'Requiem', and 'Invictus' by Bruno Hunn. There were a few more, which I can't remember, and I think I gave three broadcasts.

The accompanist for my songs was a fellow convalescent called Potter, a likeable fellow with a great sense of fun. We were conveyed to the Forces Expeditionary Station, which was at the highest point in the city, in the back of a truck operated by FANYS (ladies of the First Aid Nursing Yeomanry). There were always several girls in attendance, and our progress through Algiers was jolly.

Our convalescent camp was in a pine forest on the sea-shore. We were away from military action, but we had formidable protagonists in the camp – sand

15

fleas, which feasted on us for the whole period of my five months stay, in spite of the importation of high anti-snake beds. The chap next to me never got bitten and one or two others escaped. I don't know why. I myself was never without 60 bites! We hung our blankets out at night and morning and picked off the fleas as they emerged into the sunlight, halting their careers in a tin-lid of paraffin.

During this period I was walking in Algiers in a fairly deserted street, and around the corner amazingly came the chap who had been head boy and soloist in the church choir when I first joined, and whose best man I was destined to be in the post-war era. At that time he had a lady opera singer in tow. He was a pianist, and I recall an evening of song at her apartment. I also recall another evening there when the bailiffs were in, laying siege to the furniture. My friend and I were called upon by the lady and her mother to shift stuff from one room to another in advance of the bailiffs. We did a pretty good job.

There came the time when my company commander, who was in Italy, heard me on the radio and decided that if I was fit enough to broadcast I was fit enough to resume my duties in Italy. It was true, but I had needed all the five months' convalescence to get back to full fitness. In fact I was finally very fit indeed, the result of much running, swimming and very violent ad hoc water polo.

Anyway, with these experiences behind me, I obeyed the summons of my Commanding Officer and rejoined my unit in Italy. This entailed travelling 400 miles across Algeria to Oran, by rail in a truck labelled 'Vingt hommes ou huit chevaux'. The horse-muck had just been swept out (well nearly). I was placed in charge of twenty Italian P.O.W.s, all of them quite docile, helping me into a moving train at one point, after I had unsuccessfully chased an Arab around a village in an effort to retrieve a greatcoat he had purloined.

There were other experiences in wartime, which could not be classified as third programme material. There were renditions of 'Bless 'em all', with unkind references to Sergeants and W.O.1s. and the Quarter-master's Stores, in the olive groves at Sousse, where vino dispensed from five-gallon petrol cans inspired the company initially to vocal virtuosity, undoubtedly rocking several hectares of Tunisian soil, but ultimately producing more mayhem than music.

In Italy, after that country's capitulation, the attachment to my section for traffic control duties of an Italian unit, with a piano-accordion playing sergeant-major, substantially boosted the standard of sing-songs. Justly or unjustly, the Italians had acquired a reputation for being poor warriors, but they certainly could be 'multo passionato' in song.

Another little outlet was at a village called Castiglione where, after a few glasses of vino in one of the cafés, I would render 'Largo al Factotum', in English, encouraged by Italian drinkers, all of whom seemed to be opera buffs. Later I was able to see a performance of *Il Barbière di Seviglia* in Ancona.

Having decided to restrict this narrative to matters musical, I find that I have spanned in a few paragraphs, six years of my life, which constituted a kind of lifetime in itself, so different from the years before and the years after, years that uncovered for me a considerable portion of life's rich tapestry - adventure, danger, comradeship, responsibility, illness, tragedy, and knowledge of other countries and people. All of these aspects of life are recorded in my personal book of experiences, but the volume is stored away in the memory bank, opened only when reference is apt. The rest of life's book is regarded as 'before' and 'after'.

Final release from the army came in March 1946, with an ensuing period of great frustration in gearing myself to clerical work after six years of outdoor work on motorcycle and in Jeep, in charge of 'sixteen men and a cook'.

Music came to my rescue. The church choir was no longer to fulfil my need, however. A couple of visits persuaded me that things were not as they were before the war. The parson (a new one since pre-war days) quite obviously was not interested in adding any vocal music to that contained in hymns and responses. This was not enough for me.

Happily, a violinist friend Tom Birchenough, who played chamber music with friends at his home, asked me to add vocal contributions. I enjoyed those evenings, which were always concluded by a visit to Thorpe Gardens Public House (later named The Boat and Bottle after 'modernisation' and now re-designed, possibly with the same glossy up-market interior).

Tom and his wife were charming hosts. Tom was a positive encyclopaedia of musical knowledge. Herbert Hood, playing 'cello, never played without smoking his pipe, although I suppose he must have been naked-mouthed at orchestral performances. I strongly suspect however that he had his pipe hooked to the 'cello bridge for occasional sorties. He was a phlegmatic but very genial character, if the reader will permit the apparent contradiction. John Underhill was serious, meticulous, conscientious, dependable and a good pianist. All three of these friends have now departed, and are hopefully playing in a higher echelon.

In 1947 my life took a different turning. The County Council staff in those days was keen on social events. One such event was to be a dance, and the organiser invited staff to contribute to a cabaret, which was to follow the dance. I auditioned with 'Largo al Factotum' (in Italian now), and was accepted. Also accepted was a very attractive young lady who sang, 'We'll gather lilacs'. That lady was one called Audrey Woolsey who within a very short space of time was to become my wife. After this meeting I dated her. Audrey contends that I proposed on that night. I don't think I could possibly have been so impetuous. I think it was about four days afterwards.

The winter of 1946/47 was one of the worst on record, with roads snowed up and those, which were cleared, caked with ice. My ardour must have been pretty considerable, because I travelled regularly on my Triumph Speed Twin motorcycle from Thorpe to Wymondham to pay homage, suffering many falls, and a fine for speeding. It should be said that in those days and in early married days, Audrey as pillion passenger suffered a few falls with me.

Our marriage at Wymondham Abbey in August 1947 has worked out perfectly, with our joint interest in singing and in other directions persisting from that day to this.

My records of musical performances show little activity in 1947 and 1948. We were living with my parents, as so many young married couples were obliged to do in those early post-war years. I know that musical evenings at Thorpe continued, and that Audrey and I became close friends of John Underhill and his charming gentle wife Violet. John would accompany us in songs and oratorios, which we were learning, and later on he was our regular accompanist at concerts, for some time.

One event, which I remember was a recital which Audrey and I gave at St. John's Methodist Church at Attleborough. The organist who arranged the concert and who accompanied us at the organ was Noel Watson, (the man I met in Algiers, remember?). He was also re-established in civil life, soon to be married, with me reciprocating as best man in which office he had recently acted for me.

I recall Noel's first visit to our house after the war, made memorable by his calling my Alsatian dog Prince, which was the name we teased him with. His name was Major, and Noel was flirting with death. Happily, my reflexes were in good trim.

In a recent year, I dedicated myself to compiling a list of public performances to which Audrey and I had contributed, as a record for the family archives. This exercise evoked so many memories of people and places, that I have resolved to continue this record of musical memories, by prefacing each year with a list of the musical events with which we were concerned, and then adding such comment as the memory bank has retained, and of sufficient interest, one hopes, to entertain others. The list excludes many performances of which there is no recorded information, but includes those, which from time to time either of us has recollected, with an approximation of the year.

Up to now, I have given no biographical details of Audrey's earlier singing career. I do know however that at thirteen years of age she was performing at school concerts (monologues and songs) and at fourteen gave her first public performance at Hempnall church, singing amongst other things 'He was despised' from Handel's *Messiah*. She looks back now in wonderment at this precociousness. During the war she joined a concert party organised by the Norfolk Committee for the Entertainment of the Troops, and sang at various airfields, and at dinners.

After the war she had taken regular singing lessons with Percival Griffiths, well known in those days as a singing teacher and excellent pianist.

And so to the post-war years of increasing involvement. Audrey and I were almost invariably engaged jointly for performances where both contralto and bass or baritone were required, and for more than the next thirty years we were kept busy.

Many of the people whom I shall mention in these memoirs have now departed this world, but I shall refrain from including this statistic in referring to them, for fear that my chronicle might resemble the obituary notices in the local press.

Chapter 2 - 1949

My first oratorio performance was of Mendelssohn's *Elijah* at Silver Road Baptist Church. This was at the instigation of John Underhill (mentioned earlier). The other soloists were Edwin Kennedy (tenor), Charlotte Pank (soprano) and Hilda Riches (contralto). The choir was conducted by Leonard Allen, who was also at that time conductor of the Norwich Girls' Choir. John Underhill played the organ accompaniment. I think we all sang well. Dad was in the audience, and I recall that although he approved, he thought I should have shown more facial animation (fair comment which I remembered in later performances). There is no doubt that a composer's intentions cannot be fully interpreted with a 'dead-pan' face.

John Underhill

Chapter 3 – 1950

The Yeomen of the Guard. (Dereham Memorial Hall) ~ Recital (Music House Norwich) ~ Concert (North Elmham Institute) ~ *Messiah* (Dereham Parish Church) ~Concert (Church Hall, Holt) ~ Carol Concert (Church Rooms, North Walsham)

In 1950, Ted Barnell produced *Yeomen of the Guard* at Dereham Memorial Hall for the Dereham Evening Institute Choral Society. 'Barney' had known Audrey in earlier days (his wife had been her schoolteacher) and he knew her potential as a singer and character actress. She was cast as Dame Carruthers, and I was persuaded (rather reluctantly I think, since I had previously had no ambition to act) to take the part of Sergeant Meryll.

Bill Walden-Mills was the director of the Music House Orchestra. Mabel ('Bobbie) Roberts (soon to become Mrs Walden-Mills) was our rehearsal pianist. This was our first experience of singing with an orchestra, and the experience was thrilling. I have heard the overture to *The Yeomen* many times since then, and each hearing brings back the atmosphere of that first operatic venture. Bill was an ex-Kneller Hall man, and at that time deputy County Musical Adviser.

Amongst other contributors to solo roles with whom we maintained late contact were Harold Mould, Edwin Kennedy, Norman Abbot, Rosemarie McCombie and Jean Rudderham. Barney himself played Point. I believe this was a pretty strong cast. The chorus was strong too. The orchestra included Tom Birchenough and Herbert Hood, of whom I have written earlier, and many players with whom we would perform in later years.

The Dereham days were memorable to me not only for the singing and acting experience. After rehearsals in the schoolroom at Dereham Junior School, we would repair to the local pub, always referred to as 'Gulley's', since that enigmatic gentleman was the landlord. Gulley would occasionally disappear for weeks on end, leaving his wife to manage the pub, apparently giving no notice of his intention to do so and no indication as to his whereabouts. So far as I can remember, his wife came to accept these lapses. We stayed at this pub to amazingly late hours (sometimes the local police sergeant would join us!). I remember one occasion when we listened to the radio commentary on the fight in which Randolph Turpin won the world middleweight title.

Sometimes we would race home, competing against Bill Mills in our 1939 Ford Anglia, which we called 'Olive' because of its wartime khaki camouflage. Maximum speed without breaking the vehicle to pieces would have been about 50 mph. The Norwich to Dereham road in those days was very narrow and twisting, but deserted at that time of night. There were no breathalyser tests in those days, but I like to think that if we were young today we would act responsibly in the vastly different road conditions.

SIR RICHARD CHOLMONDELEY ... ... (Lieutenant of the Tower)		Harold Mould
COLONEL FAIRFAX (under the sentence of death)		Edwin Kennedy
SERGEANT MERYLL (of the Yeomen of the Guard)		Robert Yates
LEONARD MERYLL (his son)		Victor Morse
JACK POINT (a strolling Jester)		Edward W. Barnell
WILFRED SHADBOLT ... ... (Head Jester and Assistant Tormentor)		Norman Abbott
THE HEADSMAN		Hugh Wallis-Hosken
FIRST YEOMAN		John Lambdin
SECOND YEOMAN		Wallace Stoakley
FIRST CITIZEN		Donald Baker
SECOND CITIZEN		Lionel Fanthorpe
ELSIE MAYNARD (a strolling Singer) ...		Rosemary McCombie
PHŒBE MERYLL (Sergeant Meryll's daughter)		Jeanne Rudderham
DAME CARRUTHERS (Housekeeper to the Tower)		Audrey Yates
KATE (her neice)		Joan Seaman

Chorus of Yeomen of the Guard, Gentlemen, Citizens, etc.

LADIES OF THE CHORUS:

Irene Adams, Ida Arnell, Janet Brown, Daphne Bowles, Ethel Callaghan, Catherine Chambers, Betty Fursdon, Barbara Houseago, Joan Howard, Patricia Jones, Olive Larwood, Maureen Lemmon, Margaret Monument, Ella Oldfield, Molly Robertson, Audrey Tibbenham, Rose Wier

GENTLEMEN OF THE CHORUS :—

Cyril Bennett, John Bowden, Paul Hopkins, Ridley Larwood, Robert Mantripp, Bernard Robertson, A. M. Pryde, Percy Squires, John Thaxton, Leonard Vince

Produced by :
EDWARD W. BARNELL

Musical Director :
W. H. WALDEN-MILLS, L.R.A.M., A.R.C.M.

SCENE : TOWER GREEN
Date : 16th Century

Stage Management :	*Publicity Agent :*
R. Mantripp & John Rickword	Norman C. Vince
Wardrobe Mistresses :	*Costumes by :*
Patricia Jones and Rose Wier	Fox

Programme for *Yeomen of the Guard* at Dereham, 1950

I performed a song recital at the Music House, King Street, now part of the Wensum Lodge complex. These recitals were organised by the Music House Guild. This existed (quoting their words) 'for the purpose of presenting the more intimate forms of artistic expression under conditions so admirably provided by the Music House (*circa* 1000 A.D.). To retain a truly Norfolk character in this traditional home of music, where the finest local artists, whose activities form the backbone of our musical culture, are intermingled with more eminent international performers.'

The programme for that day shows that I was singing in the company of Rhoda Fagan, verse speaker, and Mary Barham-Johnson, harp. These two ladies were well known for their artistry. Unbelievably, I sang songs to harp accompaniment, songs which I cannot recall singing, although the programme says I did, and I must have learned them to sing from memory, since this was always a 'must' with me. Whether I sang well or badly I cannot recall, but it would have extracted the same 'Bravo's from Lesli Kurl (up-market for Leslie Curl) clad in an all-black ensemble including roll-necked pullover. One hoped that the response of the audience was engendered by their own assessment rather than by intimidation.

Leslie Curl was the catalyst for these performances, and seemed also to be a sort of janitor, for he lived in a little semi-slum behind the Theatre, which apartment served also as a Green Room. For refreshments we would repair to the Paston Room below. At performances, Leslie would appear to introduce the programmes. Performers would emerge from 'The Green Room' on to a high stage, lit by oil-lamps which would immediately dry the mucous membrane and leave one dry-mouthed, and looking into the black abyss of the 20-seat auditorium.

Perhaps this is the time to tell you a little more about Leslie. He was a frustrated musician. When stationed in South Africa during the war, he had composed a *Johannesburg Symphony*, which had met with some acclaim there, but which he had been unable to promote in this country. The fact weighed heavily upon him, and his South African Press critiques were plastered around the fireplace of a cottage he later owned at Brundall. Audrey and I were invited over there one evening to join a few other friends to listen to a recording of Bach's B Minor Mass on his new hi-fi equipment. The cottage had two adjoining rooms with no door between. We his guests, including a pleasant lady friend (unusual for Leslie) and Clifford Butler, then editor of the *Norwich Mercury* (when it was a real newspaper), listened to the records at an output of deafening decibels, whilst Leslie perched himself in the adjoining room away from the apparatus. Knowing Leslie's temperament, none of us was prepared to ask him to turn down the volume. At the end of play, Leslie emerged and waxed eulogistic about the performance. We then had some refreshments, which had been prepared by his young friend John (whom we had not seen until then), after which we nattered about music for some time. John had disappeared, and Leslie also departed, but later returned and said 'John thinks you're a lot of bloody snobs, and can talk only about music'. Duly chastened, we invited John to join us, and we talked about Norwich City Football Club and football in general until 2 a.m. You could never be safe with Leslie. For a few years we exchanged Christmas cards, and when we defaulted one year, he sent us a very stiff reprimand.

The Elmham & District Choral Society, later to become the East Norfolk Choral Society, invited Rosemarie McCombie and me to sing at their Annual Concert as soloists in Bach's *Peasant Cantata*. We also sang solos in the second half of the programme. The musical director and conductor was Edwin Kennedy. Edwin was a big man with a florid complexion, which evolved through brick-red and scarlet to purple as he imposed his vociferous and bodily energy on to his pliant chorus.

Looking at the *Messiah* programme of the performance in Dereham church, I discovered that Edwin was singing the tenor role. He was a useful tenor and Audrey and I would sing with him and under his baton on many a future occasion. We remember his wife Doreen with great affection. We were privileged to meet Doreen again recently (as I write it is after some 35 years). Now widowed, she was spending a few days with some mutual musical friends.

In this year we moved house from Thorpe to Old Costessey, and my father, a widower since my mother's departure in 1949, came with us. He lived with us until his demise in 1965, and during those years we were most fortunate to have his services as baby-sitter and later on as a child-minder. Were it not for this amenity, we could not have pursued our singing careers in the way we did, so often in tandem.

It must have been in this year that we decided to take singing lessons from Mrs Truman of Salhouse, which undertaking we were to pursue for about ten years. She taught by the York-Trotter method, and concentrated most of all on 'placing the voice'. We learned a lot in those days, but have realised since then that there was a lot she did not teach. Audrey would sing while I sat in the inglenook and chatted to husband Harry who was an architect to the War Claims Commission, and seldom appeared without pipe in mouth. Then I would emerge from the inglenook, usually banging my head in doing so, and would sing whilst Audrey sat, and finally we would be regaled with sandwiches and coffee.

We survived traumatic car journeys when, through impecuniosity, we would run out of petrol and have to push the car home. For one of those years, our transport was a Bond mini-car (a three wheeler with the engine mounted on the single front wheel, and driven by a chain which had a propensity for coming off and could only be tightened by using the biggest spanner in Norfolk, owned and kept by the garage who sold us the car). I can recall one particular wet evening when, returning from Salhouse, I lay on my back in puddles to replace the chain eleven times.

A concert at Holt included Bill Walden-Mills and Mabel (Bobbie) Roberts (both mentioned earlier). It was around this time that Bill was lodging with us at Yarmouth Road, Thorpe. A little later on, when Bobbie became Mrs Mills, we housed them both; and whilst staying with us Bobbie presented Bill with a daughter. Bobbie had previously lived in Princes Street with her parents, and when she moved into our house, some of her furniture came with her. Her father directed the removal men on how each piece should be handled, presiding at doorways, stairs and bedrooms. The forbearance of those removal men merited recognition in the Honours list.

A carol concert at North Walsham included Vaughan Williams's *Fantasia on Christmas Carols* for baritone soloist, chorus and orchestra, a work which I have enjoyed singing on several occasions.

Chapter 4 - 1951

Patience (Dereham Memorial Hall) ~ Recital (Music House, Norwich) ~ *H.M.S. Pinafore* (Theatre Royal, Norwich) ~*Bonaventure* (Thorpe Players Roxley Village Hall, Thorpe) ~ *Elijah* (North Walsham Church) ~ *Iolanthe* (Dereham Memorial Hall) ~ *Creation* (Silver Road Baptist Church, Norwich) ~ *Creation* (Old Meeting House, Norwich) ~ Concert (North Walsham School)

Our first assignment in this year was *Patience*, when Audrey was cast as Lady Jane, and I as Grosvenor. Audrey's main solo included the words 'Fading is the figure trim, spreading is the tapered waist, there will be much more of me in the coming bye and bye'. Very appropriate because this was January and Audrey was expecting Elizabeth in July. 'Barney' played Bunthorne in superb aesthetic style, and the cast and chorus included many of those who performed in *The Yeomen*. Ray Tibbenham played the Duke of Dunstable and his wife Audrey played The Lady Angela (more of these two later).

Dereham and District Amateur Operatic Society in *Patience*, 1951

The Music House Guild (president Edward Rubbra – general factotum Lesli Kurl) again requested my assistance, standing in this time for Albert Gerrard (cathedral bass) who had lost his voice. I was accompanied by Eunice Angus Phillips. She was also playing with Raymond Hasse, violin, and Edward James, 'cello in a couple of piano trios. Raymond Hasse was a professional alias for Len Calloway, with whom we shared many a concert in later years.

Bill Mills persuaded me to join the Norfolk and Norwich Amateur Operatic and Dramatic Society, and audition for the role of Captain Corcoran in *HMS Pinafore*, which they were to perform in June. Audrey was out of the running because of the impending 'event'; otherwise she would have been auditioning for Little Buttercup. I was given the part, and was in company with a number of singers with whom we have shared many a musical experience since then. In future years in fact our association with other performers, singers, pianists, instrumentalists, producers and musical directors, was to become extremely wide-spread, making it necessary to refrain from mentioning everyone for fear this narrative would become simply a catalogue of names. Nevertheless, some occasions recall memories and anecdotes, which inevitably involve fellow performers.

H.M.S.Pinafore, Captain Corcoran and Little Buttercup

In *HMS Pinafore* for instance, the cast included Harry Balders, who was such an excellent archetypal Gilbert and Sullivan 'patter man', Eric Hartley as a spine-chilling Dick Dead-Eye, Alec Forbes-Wright as a spruce Sergeant of marines and Geoffrey Oxley, later a BBC news reader, as a very sprightly midshipman. Geoffrey is the son of Louis and Ivy Oxley, then the bulwarks of the society. Bill Mills was conducting with ram-rod stance and military precision as befitted his Kneller Hall training. The producer was a Mr Bell, (domiciled in London). The programme shows his Christian name as Thomas, but I can never recollect anyone using it. Times have changed. Nevertheless, he was a very kindly man and, I think, a good producer. During one of the performances, the pistol which Ralph Rackstraw was to pick up in his 'suicide' threat was the wrong side of the backdrop and urgent efforts by stage hands to correct this situation were unavailing. The ever-resourceful Alec Ward, playing Ralph, mimed a hanging instead. The final performance was a glittering affair, since this was Festival of Britain year. All the local dignitaries were present, and I was asked to sing 'Rule Britannia' at the final curtain.

Audrey was getting bigger, and a picture we have of the play *Bonaventure* by Thorpe Players, to which we contributed, shows to what extent.

We have retained no programme of the *Elijah* at North Walsham church in that year, but although Audrey was nearing her time and not singing, she came as audience, with Audrey Tibbenham. On the way there she was sick, resulting in our late arrival at North Walsham church, in spite of flogging 'Olive', our car. A local dignitary was standing outside the church waiting for us and looking distinctly peeved. We bustled in; choir and orchestra were in position. I removed my overcoat and left it at the back of the church, sat down and immediately stood up to sing 'As God the Lord of Sabbaoth Liveth...'

Iolanthe with the Dereham Society came next. In July Audrey had produced our first born, Elizabeth. She was weaned by December and with assistance given by parent, as outlined earlier, Audrey was able to take the role of the Fairy Queen. (In the pre-natal era, the necessarily somewhat formidable interpretation would have been given 'body' as well as 'vocal' weight) Mark you, she gave a formidable interpretation. I was cast as Strephon, not wanting the role, but because this was where I had to be fitted into the casting mosaic. I was not a good Strephon, finding it hard to act as 'half-a-fairy', which led to a kind of rebellion against the producer's instructions. Later stage experience would have enabled me to assume the interpretation expected of me. The role of Lord Mountararat was the one I coveted, but this was admirably taken by Harold Mould (partnered as Lord Tolloller, by Edwin Kennedy). The Lord Chancellor was Norman Abbott, excellent in the Martyn Green tradition, although only sustaining his nerves by quite substantial intake of both alcohol and nicotine. Kathleen Rose was a lovely Phyllis. I wonder what happened to her. Musical direction was by Bill Mills, production by Ted Barnell.

At a performance of Haydn's *Creation* at the Silver Road Baptist Church (home of my baptism in singing oratorio) 'Bobby' (Charlotte) Pank sang the soprano role. Audrey and I enjoyed a long association with Bobby and husband

John. Although not singing now, she then had a magnificent voice, particularly suited to oratorio singing. The performance was repeated in December at the Old Meeting House.

A concert at North Elmham, when Audrey sang eight songs, completed the year's engagements.

This might be the right moment to mention one branch of the unrecorded performances we gave, i.e. singing at dinners. They helped the family exchequer and satisfaction came mainly from singing well (as I hope we did).

Some of these occasions involving us both were fun however. For some years we sang at the Piscators' annual dinner at the Bell Hotel, Norwich. We would sit outside the dining room on the first floor until after the toast to the Queen had been accomplished. During this waiting time we would be regaled with gin and tonic. After the toast, the door would open and a phalanx of heavy men would descend the adjacent stairway, heavy with intent. Having done what they intended to do they would mount the stairway breathing stertorously, take their seats and in we would go, like sacrificial lambs. The chairman would announce us, sometimes with difficulty, whilst swaying gently. On one occasion for instance he welcomed us 'most votefully'. On these occasions, and assisted by the afore-mentioned G & Ts we would adopt a light-hearted attitude. I remember that on one occasion Audrey lost her words. With mercurial presence of mind she said: 'Gentlemen, if you lose your bait, you bait again. Having lost my words, I'll start again'. She had sobered sufficiently to get it right the second time, evoking great applause. I remember on that same night, I finally jumped on to a table and led them in community singing.

Masons were always good audiences (I am *not* a Mason), but the room was always smoke-filled which provided another element to battle against. Here again, before performing (on my own on these occasions) I would wait in an adjoining room, listening to the various thumpings (one day I will get a Mason to explain), fending off sleep with difficulty, and then be called in when the knocking stopped.

Chapter 5 - 1952

Coffee Cantata (Assembly House, Norwich) ~ ***Bastien and Bastienne*** (Assembly House, Norwich) ~ ***Acis and Galatea*** (Assembly House, Norwich) ~ ***Pirates of Penzance*** (Theatre Royal, Norwich) ~ ***Cox and Box*** (Theatre Royal, Norwich) ~ Recital (Music House, Norwich) ~ ***Beggar's Opera*** (Maddermarket Theatre, Norwich)

The double-bill of *Coffee Cantata* (Bach) and *Bastien and Bastienne* (Mozart) at the Assembly House, was a delight. In 1952 the Music Room was not carpeted and resonance was good. Apart from the music, I shall always remember the magnificence of Eric Hartley processing the length of the Music Room, with a tray of drinks held high. I remember too, that in the *Coffee Cantata*, Ivy Oxley, whom I have mentioned in the context of Theatre Royal performances, was my daughter, despite being in actual life quite a few years my senior. In *Bastien and Bastienne*, which Mozart wrote at the age of eleven, I played Colas the magician, achieving things that I have never been able to achieve in real life. These were ventures presented jointly by Sidney Twemlow and Jack Mitchley, then County Music advisor and County Drama advisor respectively.

Another presentation by Sidney Twemlow was a concert version of Handel's *Acis and Galatea*, which is classified variously as a masque, semi-opera or pastoral opera, though I have never seen it presented as such. Looking at the programme, I observe that the chorus was the Norfolk and Norwich Bach choir. I have said that it would be tedious to mention every name, but lest I omit them

Box and Cox, 1952

28

in later pages, let me remember here, with affection, and because we shared so many occasions with them, the names of John McKenna and Arthur Hedges, oboe and flute respectively. They were real professionals, who on this occasion were joined by other extremely talented musicians, constituting the small chamber orchestra, which accompanied the singers.

Audrey was back in action again for *Pirates of Penzance* where she took the unlovable role of Ruth (heavily disguised, I might add, to bring verisimilitude to the character). *Cox and Box* made up a double bill, and I played Cox, a role I much enjoyed.

Pirates of Penzance

In May, I sang again at the Music House, with the Music House Singers and Players. Here again, I cannot recall these performers ever appearing again under that title. The Players element was represented by John Bacon, a very talented young violinist, with whom Audrey and I shared many a performance thereafter.

The Beggars' Opera was presented in December, and was a joint venture between the Norfolk and Norwich Amateur Operatic Society and the Maddermarket Players, a collaboration that I think had never been attempted before. The Players took the speaking parts of The Beggar and The Player. The opera was directed by Nugent Monck, who founded the Maddermarket Trust way back. He was a nationally renowned personality, of whom others are more qualified to speak than I. It was Nugent Monck's swan song, and it seemed an unusual choice, since one would have expected him to have chosen something exclusive to Norwich Players. However, it was a privilege to be directed by the great man. I enjoyed the role of Captain Macheath as well as, possibly more, than any other role I have played, and happily it was one that I was able to play on several future occasions. Audrey was a splendid Mrs Peachum, and Peachum and Lockitt were played by Harold Mould and Eric Hartley, with such vigour one marvels that the stage could have withstood the disputations, sometimes physical, between these two large men.

***The Beggar's Opera* 1952, at the Maddermarket**
By courtesy of Eastern Counties Newspapers

The Beggar's Opera, 1952

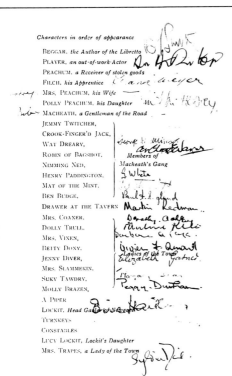

Characters in order of appearance

BEGGAR, *the Author of the Libretto*
PLAYER, *an out-of-work-Actor*
PEACHUM, *a Receiver of stolen goods*
FILCH, *his Apprentice*
MRS. PEACHUM, *his Wife*
POLLY PEACHUM, *his Daughter*
MACHEATH, *a Gentleman of the Road*
JEMMY TWITCHER,
CROOK-FINGER'D JACK,
WAT DREARY,
ROBIN OF BAGSHOT, *Members of*
NIMMING NED, *Macheath's Gang*
HENRY PADDINGTON,
MAT OF THE MINT,
BEN BUDGE,
DRAWER AT THE TAVERN
MRS. COAXER,
DOLLY TRULL,
MRS. VIXEN,
BETTY DOXY,
JENNY DIVER, *Ladies of the Town*
MRS. SLAMMEKIN,
SUKY TAWDRY,
MOLLY BRAZEN,
A PIPER
LOCKIT, *Head Gaoler of Newgate*
TURNKEYS
CONSTABLES
LUCY LOCKIT, *Lockit's Daughter*
MRS. TRAPES, *a Lady of the Town*

Scenes:

Prologue
1. Peachum's House
   A Street (*Front Scene*)
2. A Tavern

INTERVAL

3. Newgate
   A Street
4. The Tavern
   A Street
5. The Condemned Hold
6. Newgate

The Maddermarket version is by Nugent Monck and the music is arranged by Cecil Smyly.

The Overture was composed and the songs arranged from popular versions of old and contemporary airs by John Christopher Pepusch, who was born in Prussia in 1667, came to England as a young man, worked here for the rest of his life and died in 1752.

John Gay was born in Devonshire in the year 1688, and educated at the free-school of Barnstaple. He died on the 4th December, 1732, and on the 23rd December was buried in Westminister Abbey, that is 220 years ago. The Beggar's Opera was first given at Lincoln's Inn Fields Theatre on the 29th January, 1728, under the management of John Rich. Its immediate success of an uninterrupted run of 63 nights was said to have made "Gay rich and Rich gay."

Coffee (Tea at the Matinees) will be served in the Coffee Room during the Interval.

NO SMOKING IN ANY PART OF THE THEATRE OR COFFEE ROOM

The programme for *The Beggars' Opera*

Chapter 6 - 1953

Yeomen of the Guard (Theatre Royal, Norwich) ~ **St Matthew Passion**
(St Andrew's Hall, Norwich) ~ **Merrie England** (concert version)
(Memorial Hall, Dereham)W.I. Coronation Festival (St Andrew's Hall,
Norwich) ~ **Merrie England** (concert version) (Church Rooms, North
Walsham) ~ Victoriana (Sprowston Secondary Modern School) ~
Merrie England (concert version) (King Edward Vll Grammar School,
King's Lynn) ~ **Carmen** (concert version) and Songs
(Wymondham Secondary Modern School)

1953 was the year in which we became involved with Sidney Twemlow's yearly presentation of Bach's *St Matthew Passion* at St Andrew's Hall, I taking the part of Christus and Audrey singing the contralto arias. Sidney always engaged a professional singer to sing the part of the Evangelist, and sometimes professionals for other solo contributions. Over a period of eight years, we were privileged to sing with some of the world's great exponents of this work, including Peter Pears, Rene Soames, Eric Greene and Anne Wood. Audrey did not sing in this first performance because she was expecting our second daughter Julia, who arrived in October. The soprano soloist was Rita Green with whom we shared many oratorio performances in later years.

Looking at the programme for this first performance, I was staggered to note that ten Norfolk Choral Societies (including the Norfolk and Norwich Amateur Bach Choir with whom we had sung *Acis and Galatea*), totalling 315 voices, together with an orchestra of 62 players, (strings and woodwind). Sidney would rehearse each choir separately and bring them together with orchestra and soloists for a Saturday afternoon rehearsal and evening performance.

We sang the concert version of *Merrie England* at Dereham, North Walsham and King's Lynn, in this Coronation Year, and in later years were to sing it eight more times.

I was privileged to share the platform at a Coronation Festival concert at St Andrew's Hall with Lady Fermoy, who, apart from her connections with Royalty, was a concert pianist of professional status. She was very charming, as was Lady Delia Peel who organised the concert, and of whom we were to see a great deal a little later on. Sidney Twemlow was my accompanist for my group of four songs. He also conducted a performance of a cantata by Elgar entitled *The Banner of St George*, sung by the combined choirs of twenty-two Women's Institutes (soloist Sylvia Foxwell).

In the same year, I sang Escamillo in a concert version of *Carmen* at Wymondham Secondary Modern School. (Audrey was not singing Carmen on this occasion, though she did on several others). In Part II of the programme, the soloists each sang a group of songs. Looking back at the programme I observe that I am listed as singing 'Friend of Mine' (Sanderson) and 'I am a Roamer' (Mendelssohn). Either I substituted 'Largo al Factotum' for the latter song or I sang it as an encore, but I certainly sang it, irrefutably confirmed by the following incident. A lady called Winifred Allen was accompanying the soloists, but I had rehearsed with Sidney Twemlow because of the aria's complexity. Winifred turned over the music for Sidney, and at the first turn over, she whipped the music into the third row of the audience. Sidney extemporised for a while, leading me into uncharted regions, finally gave up and said 'Mr Yates, I think we had better explain to the audience what has happened'. 'I couldn't agree more', I said. I was on tenterhooks during this second rendition, because to fumble this difficult tongue-twisting Italian operatic aria now would not be humorous. We survived, and its successful completion was acknowledged by 'Good ole boy!' from the back of the hall.

Two more *Merrie England*s were demanded of us. Arthur Hedges the flautist, whom I mentioned earlier, had a pleasant tenor voice. I remember that we painted his greying beard with iodine to produce a convincing Raleigh at North Walsham. This might be the point at which to say that Arthur's wife Doreen was also a flautist (and writer and artist). In later years we purchased her flute for our daughter Julia, and later still a painting by her of St Peter Mancroft by floodlight, not knowing it to be hers because of the use of her maiden name Doreen Idle. All was revealed when we spoke to her at an exhibition at the Assembly House.

Raleigh at King's Lynn was John Ford, a young professional who had sung the Evangelist arias in Sidney Twemlow's *St Matthew Passion*. Sidney accompanied Charlotte Pank and me in Victorian songs at 'An Exhibition of Items of Interest and Value from the Reign of Queen Victoria' at Sprowston.

Yeomen of the Guard gave Audrey and myself the opportunity of playing Dame Carruthers and Sergeant Meryll once more. Opera producer, Tyrone Guthrie, once said that there is never an opera performance that is not on the verge of breakdown. This undoubtedly is true, but operas in which I have been involved have managed to avoid such disaster – sometimes only just. My memory is therefore not soured by such experiences. It is the small things that feed the memory with anecdotal material. Here is one such item: -

In our performance of *Yeomen*, the part of Leonard, Sergeant Meryll's son, was taken by a man with minimal experience in this kind of work. In the opera, Sergeant Meryll says to his daughter Phoebe: 'Thy brother Leonard, who, as a reward for his valour in saving his standard and cutting his way through fifty foes who would have hanged him, has been appointed a Yeoman of the Guard, will arrive this morning...' A little later on Leonard appears to exclaim 'Father!' Well, Leonard obviously regarded me as an experienced old hand and sought advice on how to deliver the word 'Father!' We juggled with various interpretations – surprise, joy, emotion, pragmatism etc., finally settling on a delivery, which would not bring a frown to the brow of discerning Gilbert and Sullivan devotees. At the first performance, he entered. The strain was too much! He rendered a 'Father!' that must have been the envy of all the sopranos, and indeed must have vied for power and eloquence, with the utterances of those single-minded gentlemen, who, in their youth had been 'cut off' in their prime.

Chapter 7 - 1954

Carmen (concert version) (North Walsham Church Rooms) ~ *Tom Jones* (concert version) (Dereham Memorial Hall) ~ *St Matthew Passion* (St Andrew's Hall, Norwich) ~ St Mark Passion (Diss Parish church) ~ Song recital (Maddermarket Theatre, Norwich) ~ Song recital (St George's Colegate, Norwich) ~ Song recital (St Andrew's Church, Norwich) ~ *Messiah* (Octagon Chapel, Norwich) ~ *The Bartered Bride* (concert version) (Sir John Leman School, Beccles) ~ *Messiah* (Deneside, Great Yarmouth) ~ *Christmas Cantata* (Cromer Parish Church) ~ *Messiah* (Blakeney Church) ~ *Messiah* (St Peter Mancroft Church, Norwich)

Looking at the programme of our *Carmen* production, I observe that it was conducted by John McKenna (mentioned previously) and accompanied by Winifred Allen. The fact that I sang 'None but the Lonely Heart' and 'Non Piu Andrai', with no mention of another accompanist in the programme must mean that Winifred also accompanied my songs.

Tom Jones by Edward German used to go well in concert version, and this would not be the only time we would contribute to a performance of this work. On this occasion, the choir was Elmham and District Choral Society, (later to become Mid-Norfolk Choral Society), and the accompaniment was provided by a string quartet, led by Leonard Ward, a peripatetic violin teacher employed by the Norfolk Education Department, and talented leader of many an orchestra in the county's musical presentations, notably in the *St Matthew Passion* performances, and later in the St Andrew's Hall Christmas concerts, of which more anon.

This year the Evangelist in *St Matthew Passion* was Peter Pears. Standing side by side with him was a great privilege. He was modest and unassuming, and the only thing that worried me was that in sitting down, he sat on his tails! The chorus this year mustered 309 singers, with an orchestra of 72.

At Diss Parish Church, I sang the role of Jesus, with Heddle Nash's younger son David as evangelist, in a *St Mark's Passion* by Charles Wood. David, in my estimation, would never reach the height of attainment of his illustrious father, nor of his elder brother John who had already earned a reputation in opera. It was a presentation by the Diss Choral Society. Other contributors were George Milnes who sang the four supporting bass roles in the work. I remember George as a good reliable singer. The organist was John Underhill, and the conductor Brian Douglas, then Sidney Twemlow's deputy.

The Maddermarket recital was part of a concert presented by The Ariel Singers, conductor Robert Boswell, accompanist Ena Robinson. They sang the first of the *Scenes from the Song of Hiawatha* – 'Hiawatha's Wedding Feast', and this work occupied the second half of the performance. What happened to the Ariel Singers? Audrey's and my contributions were in the first half of the programme, and our accompanist was Bernard Burrell, who was then assistant organist at Norwich Cathedral. Bernard was a dear friend and a lovely man. Regrettably his life was to be cut short.

At the recital at St George's Church we were joined by Charlotte Pank, soprano and Stanley Littlechild, tenor, and Bernard Burrell played the organ. The five of us joined forces on many occasions.

The St Andrew's Church recital was shared with Arthur Andrews, trumpet, and my contribution was of excerpts from the *Messiah*, including of course 'The Trumpet shall Sound' and 'Lord God of Abraham' from *Elijah*. Arthur played Haydn's Trumpet Concerto in E flat and an excerpt from Rheinberger's Sonata No 8. Arthur and his brother Fred were prominent local trumpet players in those days.

Messiah at the Octagon Chapel was presented by the Catton Choral Society. Proceeds from this recital were to go to the restoration fund set up for the 'repair of ravages of the death-watch beetle in the beams and rafters and the effect of 200 years wear and tear on the tiling, stone and plasterwork'. Bernard Burrell was again at the organ with Charlotte Pank, soprano and Frank Weyer sang the tenor role.

Audrey and I were greatly indebted to the Catton Choral Society for inviting us to sing with them. This provided us with the opportunity of learning the contralto and bass contributions in most of the well-known oratorio repertoire. Our introduction to that society came from an invitation by Gerald Manning, secretary of the society, and up to that time its bass soloist. Gerald wished to relinquish the bass roles, and I suppose our names must have been getting around. This experience was invaluable to us, in the many future performances with which we were to become involved. Gerald and his wife Queenie became great friends, and we were able to share in the maturing and musical development of their daughter Jane, firstly by sharing many an engagement with her and then witnessing her progress to a soprano of international repute.

At a performance of a concert version of Smetana's *The Bartered Bride* I shared the platform with Anne Pashley soprano, and her father, Roy Pashley, tenor. Anne was very young and had just decided to discontinue her athletic activities as part of the Olympic British relay team. She had decided that singing was to be her career. As I remember, she sang quite well but would need more experience to develop. The fact that she became a soloist with the Welsh National Opera is sufficient comment. Audrey and I sang with her a few times after *Bartered Bride* and found her to be a nice girl. She was always accompanied by her mother and her grandmother. It was greatly to Anne's credit that the old lady was always included in her 'entourage'.

In a performance of the *Messiah* at Deneside, Great Yarmouth, the contralto soloist was a Mandy Heaton, a member of the Covent Garden Opera Company. It was December, and she wore long combinations under her dress (I know because she showed me!) The other memorable incident from that occasion concerned the tenor Joseph Nicholson, who was a local clergyman. After afternoon rehearsal, we all changed into our evening dress attire in a side room, when it became apparent that Joseph's dress jacket was missing from its peg. Norman Cutting (the organist on this occasion, and on many another the conductor of the Sheringham and Cromer Choral Society) always spoke, when making pronouncements, in a voice, which was a cross between Edward Everet Horton and Mr Punch. He said, 'You have mine old boy, it doesn't matter if I am in mufti'. Now Norman was tall and thin, and Joseph was short and fat, but the coat fitted him perfectly. He shuffled around in embarrassment for some time, until John Pank, accompanying Bobbie (Charlotte) picked up a coat and said, 'Whose is this?' It was Norman's.

The Sheringham and Cromer Choral Society presented a cantata by Arthur Somervell entitled *Christmas*. I can't remember anything about this work, but the programme shows that I shared the solo work with Alice Peters, soprano, Edith Judd, contralto, and Frank Platford, tenor. Norman Cutting was of course conducting, and the organist was Cyril Pearce, well known for his performances at St Andrew's Hall, and throughout Norfolk.

Audrey sang the contralto arias in the *Messiah* at Blakeney Church with professional tenor Edgar Fleet, and again at St Peter Mancroft. Later, Edgar was to marry Jean Allister, a renowned mezzo-soprano.

BECCLES CHORAL SOCIETY

Presents

The Bartered Bride

A Comic Opera by FREDERIC SMETANA
(arr. Julius Harrison)

In the New Assembly Hall,
Sir John Leman School, Beccles
On Saturday, November 20th, 1954
Commencing at 7.30 p.m.

Principals :

ANNE PASHLEY   -   Soprano
ROY PASHLEY   - -   Tenor
ROBERT YATES -   - -   Bass

Chorus and Orchestra

Conductor - REGINALD FIRTH

Accompanists :
MARY FIRTH and O. LLOYD SMITH

Orchestra Leader :
IRENE UNDERWOOD

The National Federation of Music Societies (to which the Beccles Choral Society is affiliated) supports this concert with funds provided by the Arts Council of Great Britain.

Programme 6d.

Chapter 8 - 1955

Concert ~ (Lads' Club, Norwich) ~ *Creation* (Rosebery Road Methodist
Church, Norwich) ~ Song recital (Diss Corn Hall) ~ *Creation* (St Peter
Mancroft Church, Norwich) ~ Concert (Old Meeting House, Norwich)
~*The Rebel Maid* (concert version) (Dereham Memorial Hall) *Iolanthe*
(Theatre Royal, Norwich) ~ Song recital (Music House, Norwich) ~
The Bartered Bride (concert version) (Norwich Union) ~ *Creation*
(St Peter's Church, Sheringham) ~ *St Matthew Passion* (St Andrew's
Hall, Norwich) ~ Norfolk Cantata Singers (St Peter Mancroft Church,
Norwich) ~ *Beggar's Opera* (Assembly House, Norwich) ~
Messiah (Wells Parish Church) ~ Concert (Maddermarket Theatre,
Norwich) *The Rebel Maid* (concert version) (Sparrow's Nest Theatre,
Lowestoft) ~ Song recital (Old Meeting House, Norwich) ~
Tales of Hoffman (concert version) (Sir John Leman School, Lowestoft)
~ *Messiah* (Town Hall, Great Yarmouth) *Merrie England* (concert
version) (The Parish Hall, Cromer) ~ Carol Concert (Lads' Club,
Norwich) ~ Christmas Concert (St Andrew's Hall, Norwich)

Looking at the above list, it is difficult to imagine how we fitted it all in, since I
was in full-time employment, and Audrey was attendant upon our two daughters
in their early years. However, the list reveals that a number of the works
performed were solidly in the repertoire from previous performances. This
helped, although one never rested on one's laurels, but always sought
improvement. An additional factor was that, as previously recorded, my father
lived with us, and with his assistance I cannot recall that our daughters'
upbringing suffered. Later on, they took piano lessons with Joan Roe, notable
pianist in Norfolk at that time. Later still, they went to music colleges, and
although they now have other qualifications as well, they still enjoy their music.

In this year, Bernard Burrell collected a number of singers, all of soloist
status, to join together as The Norfolk Cantata Singers. We gave one
performance at St Peter Mancroft Church, but sadly this was all. It would have
been a rather splendid group if its members had stuck together, but they drifted
away to do their own thing.

The evangelist in this year's *St Matthew Passion* was René Soames,
internationally renowned, particularly for his singing of French songs. He was a
down-to-earth man as the following incident illustrates. We the soloists repaired
to the 'green room' (or Committee room as it also served) and we were joined by
the committee of the Norfolk Rural Music School. They appeared to be enjoying
themselves and took no notice of us. René Soames was grossly offended at this,
and made loudly spoken remarks the colour of which surpassed anything I had
experienced during six years of army service. Unhearing, Bishop Herbert strode
up and down in his gaiters, and the rest of the committee were far too busy
talking.

Elizabeth Bainbridge took the contralto solos this year. A beautiful singer, she was later to become an established star at Covent Garden.

The Choral Societies contributing to this performance were, Barton Turf and District, Burnham Market, Catton, Diss, Fakenham, Holt, Lowestoft, North Walsham, Sheringham and Cromer, and Wymondham.

The Diss Corn Hall recital was not without incident. Audrey and Bernard Burrell, who was my accompanist, travelled with me. On the way there our car broke down (the big end had gone). In our impecunious state, this was like being kicked in the stomach by a mule. I hitched a lift on the back of a motor-cycle to Dickleborough, dress coat-tails flying. I purchased a gallon of oil and returned with it, courtesy of the generous motor-cyclist. We limped into Diss and arrived just in time to hear Jessie Hall (with whom I shared the recital) finish a Beethoven sonata. It was a stern test of memory, and diaphragmatic support in these circumstances, particularly since several of the songs were very dramatic 'first-timers'. However, all went well. The sickness of heart reinstated itself on the way home. Not being able to afford a new engine, we had to buy a motor-bike.

We performed *The Beggar's Opera* again, this time at the Assembly House (The Hellesdon Opera Group). Jane Manning, of whom I have spoken, was a chorus member, and had, I later learned, formed a 'Robert Yates (or was it a Captain Macheath?) fan club at Norwich High School, which she still attended. They gave vociferous support.

The Rebel Maid at Lowestoft and *The Tales of Hoffman* at Beccles introduced me to four more top-ranking professionals in Gwen Catley (remember her in the radio programme 'Round the Horn'?) George Allen, Adrienne Cole and Edgar Fleet (who had sung with Audrey in the earlier *Messiah*).

Then there was a *Messiah* at the Town Hall, Great Yarmouth, with the City of Norwich School Orchestra. This was the first of many appearances there, and the occasion was memorable for the fact that the central heating (always generous) had induced me to doze off momentarily, just before 'Why do the Nations'. Apparently Audrey, who sat next to me on the stage, heard a slight snore. She nudged me, and I responded, but not before the introductory music had started. Those of you who are familiar with the aria will know the physical effort involved.

The Town Hall engagements were always most agreeable, because the hall itself had splendid acoustic properties and architectural splendour. Moreover, we always had sherry with the Town Mayor during the interval.

Merrie England at Cromer was notable for the fact that Geraldine Barber, who was to have sung the contralto and mezzo roles was unable to do so because of illness, and Audrey deputised without rehearsal. The orchestra was led by Sidney Gould, who was the long-established leader of the Norwich Philharmonic Orchestra; the conductor was of course Norman Cutting.

I see from my archives that in the performance of *The Bartered Bride,* and for the recital at the Music House, the accompanist was Joan Brooks. She was a splendid pianist, and her sister Daisy Brooks, whom we were to meet in a later year, was a nationally renowned miniaturist.

The first of the two concerts at the Lads' club was in January and was in aid of the Fire Disaster Appeal Fund. (The disaster was a fire in the Lads' Club itself). The concert was presented by the Norwich Amateur Rowing Association, and its contributors included Sydney Grapes, that well-known Norfolk entertainer, and The Norwich Singers conducted by Roy Henton. I do recall that the acoustics were reminiscent of those at the St Augustine's swimming pool.

The second concert was a Community Carol Concert in December. Audrey and Charlotte Pank contributed to this.

I remember that *Iolanthe* at The Theatre Royal was produced by a gentleman who had finished a week's production of variety at the Norwich Hippodrome (yes, it was still standing in 1955). I believe that he had little experience of producing a Gilbert and Sullivan Opera, made manifest by the minimum instruction meted out to both chorus and soloists. The press was kind however, so it couldn't have been too bad. I remember particularly the fun we had in the famous trio (Lord Chancellor – Harry Balders, Lord Tolloller – Alexander Ward and Lord Mountararat – yours truly).

The song recitals listed were two of many presented by four of us whose friendship grew from our joint participation as soloists in works performed by various Norfolk and Suffolk Choral Societies. Audrey and I were accompanied on these occasions by Charlotte Pank and Stanley Littlechild, Bernard Burrell and John Underhill.

Left to right: AudreyYates, Stanley Littlechild, Charlotte Pank, John Underhill, Bob Yates. Bernard Burrell is at the piano.

The Christmas Concert was a new venture of Sidney Twemlow, which was to continue until 1965. This presentation included Part 1 of the *Messiah* and carols for choir and audience. The Choral Societies on this occasion included Heacham, North Elmham, Upton, Diss, Holt, Litcham, North Walsham, Upton and Wymondham and the Church choirs of Hethersett, Princes Street, Norwich, Spooner Row and Sprowston. The County Orchestra was led by Leonard Ward.

Chapter 9 - 1956

Mr Pepys (Assembly House, Norwich) ~ Concert (Assembly House, Norwich) ~ Concert (Chapelfield Methodist Church, Norwich) ~ *Elijah* (Dereham Road Baptist Church, Norwich) ~ Concert (Toc H, Loddon) ~ *St Matthew Passion* (St Andrew's Hall, Norwich) ~ Recital (Strumpshaw Church) ~ *Creation* (St Mary's Baptist Church, Norwich) ~ Concert (St Andrew's Hall, Norwich) ~ *Messiah* (St John's Church, Lowestoft) ~ Festival of Remembrance (Hippodrome Theatre, Great Yarmouth) ~ *Fantasia on Christmas Carols* (Horning Church) ~ *Christmas Oratorio* (St Peter's Church, Sheringham) ~ Christmas Concert (St Andrew's Hall, Norwich) ~ Concert (St Andrew's Hall, Norwich) ~ Carol Concert (Lads' Club, Norwich)

We gave a staged performance of Martin Shaw's ballad opera *Mr Pepys* at the Assembly House. Audrey and Jane Manning sang together in a duet, which won acclaim from Martin Shaw himself, then over 90, who was in the audience. I didn't make a good Mr Pepys. I think I sang well enough, but perhaps remained a bit too much like myself. Jane tells me that Martin Shaw's grandson; Robert Shaw was her producer/director in a recent performance.

Richard Butt was Sidney Twemlow's deputy in this year and was also conducting performances by the Norfolk and Norwich Operatic Society. He asked me to sing the baritone solo in Vaughan Williams *Fantasia on Christmas Carols* at Horning Church. When the performance date arrived, dense fog blanketed the whole of the county – fog the likes of which is never encountered in these days of houses without chimneys. At five o'clock, I went across from my working base at 29 Thorpe Road, to 22 Stracey Road, the home of the County Education Music dept. and asked Richard if the performance was still on. He confirmed that it was and said that if I didn't want to use my car I could travel with him and his two passengers. I hastened to convey as politely as possible that anything he could do I could do better. Mark you he had two passengers to put their heads out of windows, whereas I had to make my own decisions. It was this factor that led me into someone's garden at Hoveton and later to be overtaken by Richard and company whilst I was trying to read a signpost. Independent still, I waved him on.

The archives reveal that Audrey and I contributed to several concerts during the year, joining forces variously with Charlotte Pank, soprano, Frank Weyer, tenor, Bernard Wesby, tenor, Lawrence Mallyon, bass, Tom Birchenough, violin, Joan Brooks and Joan Roe, piano, Norwich Singers, and others whose performances perhaps marked the only occasion on which we met. The price of the Chapelfield programme is shown as 3d.

We took a comparatively classical repertoire to the Loddon concert, only to find that the front row was occupied by small children sucking ice-creams. Bernard Wesby and I decided to alter things a bit by singing 'The Gendarmes

Duet', jumping off the stage and endeavouring to strike terror into the hearts of the front row juveniles. I think they continued sucking their ice-creams.

You will see that we were involved in further repetitions of major oratorios, but I think that this was our first performance of Bach's *Christmas Oratorio*.

We contributed to The Festival of Remembrance at the Hippodrome, Great Yarmouth on 11th November. This was a moving occasion. The Hippodrome is a great place to sing in (so long as the animals are not in occupation). A circus had been performing there immediately before our concert, leaving some of the straw-filled stalls and the odour of elephants behind them. We took our highest fee to date for this performance, but our consciences were salved because of the massive fee-paying audience.

This was the second year of Sidney Twemlow's 'Christmas Concert', and we were to be involved intermittently.

Our association with the Reverend Charles Coleman began when I contributed to a performance of Stainer's *Crucifixion* in Sea Palling Church (date not recorded nor was there a programme for retention). Anyway, Charles moved to Strumpshaw where Audrey and I, and other soloists sang under his baton on sundry occasions, including this year. Charles' father, C.J.R. Coleman who was organist of St Peter Mancroft Church, would always accompany us. Charlotte Pank and Frank Weyer were again with us, in this 1957 recital. I never knew Charles' father's Christian name (things were a bit more formal in those days), but I do remember his less formal injunction upon arrival at Strumpshaw and other churches. Aware of the lack of facilities within, he would say, 'Come along Robert – the north wall'.

One of the programmes salvaged from our collection shows that Audrey was singing in a concert in aid of The Royal National Institute for the Blind. Other performers were Lawrence Mallyon, bass, John Bacon, violin, The Norwich Singers, and the Drayton and District British Legion Silver Band.

LOWESTOFT CHORAL SOCIETY

HANDEL'S

𝕸𝖊𝖘𝖘𝖎𝖆𝖍

ST. JOHNS' CHURCH - LOWESTOFT

Thursday 6th December, 1956 at 7.30 p.m.

Miss MARGARET WHIPP Soprano   Mrs. AUDREY YATES Contralto

Mr. BRADBRIDGE WHITE Tenor   Mr. ROBERT YATES Baritone

Organist   MILLARD-TOLHURST ORCHESTRA
Mr. SIDNEY MILLER   Leader J. GODDARD

Conductor CLAUDE L. RICHARDS

Admission by Programme   -   -   -   -   -   -   2/-

Chapter 10 - 1957

Broadcasts (Birmingham) ~ *St Matthew Passion* (St Andrew's Hall, Norwich) ~ *Messiah* (Fakenham Parish Church) ~ Concert (Townswomen's Guild, Town Hall, Great Yarmouth) Concert (County Light Orchestra, Sheringham) ~ *Messiah* (Shotesham Parish Church) ~ *Carmen* (concert version) (Assembly House, Norwich) ~ *Elijah* (St Mary's Baptist Church, Norwich) ~ Concert (Strumpshaw Church) ~ Recital (Octagon Chapel Norwich) ~ *Hiawatha's Wedding Feast* (Town Hall, Great Yarmouth) ~ *Christmas Oratorio* (Fakenham Parish Church) ~ *Messiah* (Christmas Concert, St Andrew's Hall, Norwich)

In 1957, I auditioned for BBC radio, presenting myself at Studio 4, Broad Street, Birmingham, together with sundry other aspirants. I was contacted later and invited to broadcast.

I travelled the day before, because the audition was at 10.45 a.m. the next morning. Getting from City Station, Norwich to New Street Station, Birmingham took about 4½ hours, with several changes. City Station is of course long demolished and its existence lost in the traffic complex at Barn Road roundabout. I shared the journey with sandwich-eating, scandal-mongering, book-devouring people, seated on long seats opposite each other, the variety changing at each stop. On the rare occasions that the compartment was empty, I rehearsed in full voice.

On arrival at New Street Station, I had to find accommodation for the night. It was late evening and all hotels and bed and breakfast establishments in the city centre seemed to be full up. I took a bus to some outlying village club (it must have been recommended to me by someone), had a drink at the bar, which amazingly was being attended by a Norwich girl, and retired to bed.

In the morning, I must have bussed in again, because I can recall pacing up and down the Civic Centre, ensuring that the voice placement was in order, lapsing into sotto voce as people passed.

In March, I was given a spot in Midland Music Club, introduced by David Franklin, renowned operatic bass, and standing 6 ft. 7 ins. with a voice so cavernous that I seemed to be speaking like a soprano. However, I mustered my best bass-baritone texture and delivered Stanford's 'The Old Superb'. My accompanist was Albert Webb, who at that time was presenting a Palm Court Orchestra on radio. His wife was present at the rehearsal and at the broadcast (which was to a studio audience) where she confided in me that Albert was not well. Not long afterwards, his death was announced. He was an extremely pleasant man and his passing was mourned by everyone at Studio 4. My broadcast was shared with well know pianists Viola Tunnard and Martin Penny who played piano duets. The production was by a Reginald Perrin! I wish I had recordings of this and subsequent broadcasts, but perhaps I would now shudder at those early efforts. Nevertheless, I must have done reasonably well, since the broadcast was the first of several.

I was offered another broadcast in August. Having experienced some difficulty in obtaining overnight accommodation in Birmingham, I decided to go by car. Audrey could come with me, and we could sleep in the car. It was a run-down Morris 12 of some vintage, but it had a bench front seat. Looking back I am incredulous that I made this decision, but money was also a consideration in those days, and by taking the car we could make a profit on fees and expenses (£7.7.0. and £4.16.4. respectively). We travelled the day before because the rehearsal was scheduled for 9.45 a.m. and the recording was to be made at 11.45 a.m. the next day. We parked in a field just outside Birmingham, with the notorious Birmingham 'smog' enveloping us. Audrey 'slept' in the front and I in the back. Although it was August, it was a chilly night and a somewhat harrowing experience. At six o'clock in the morning I ran around the field in singlet and trousers, in an effort to get the circulation going.

On this occasion, Leo Wurmser was my accompanist. He was an orchestral conductor and pianist, quite prominent at that time. I think he was Austrian. After recording, he took us to lunch in the BBC canteen. He was very short-sighted and he asked me to say whether it was his wife sitting at the other side of the canteen. After the recital, Audrey wanted to look around Birmingham, but by this time I was semi-moribund, so we set off for home, and listened to the broadcast on a portable radio in a field somewhere near Leicester.

Another *St Matthew Passion* three more *Messiahs*, and *Christmas Oratorio* at Fakenham were our 'book-in-hand' contributions in this year.

The name of organist W. E. Mowton appears in one of the *Messiah* presentations. He accompanied us on several occasions, and I have never forgotten his wise-crack about the tenor in one performance of *Messiah* who sang 'the crook, Ed Straight'. (For the uninitiated, please look at the first tenor arias).

A concert performance of *Carmen*, at the Assembly House, with the St Cecilia Chorus and orchestra was conducted by Paul Artis. Interesting to note that the assistant repetiteur was Eileen Bidwell (later to become Eileen Last, whose contributions to the local musical scene since then are myriad.) Audrey sang Carmen, Charlotte Pank Micaela, Alex (Tim) Wilson sang Don José, and I Escamillo.

The first concert at Yarmouth was with the combined Women's Guild Choirs which included those from Gorleston (evening), King's Lynn (afternoon and evening), King's Lynn Gaywood, Lowestoft (afternoon), Lowestoft (evening), Norwich Earlham, Norwich Eaton (afternoon), Norwich Eaton (evening), Norwich Central, Norwich Catton, Yarmouth (afternoon). The conductor was Mary Firth, with whom Audrey and I were associated in concerts in Beccles, which her husband Reginald Firth conducted, she then playing 'cello. The programme included *The Forsaken Merman* by Arthur Somervell, for baritone solo, women's voices and pianoforte. I found the work not exactly memorable, which rather put me off Arthur Somervell, until in later years I came across his setting of some of A. E. Housman's *The Shropshire Lad* poems, which I enjoy.

The second concert at Great Yarmouth was a double-bill of Coleridge Taylor's *Hiawatha's Wedding Feast* a cantata for tenor voice and chorus, and

Ralph Vaughan-Williams' *Fantasia on Christmas Carols* for baritone soloist and choir. The choruses were sung by the Great Yarmouth Musical Society, conducted by Cyril Huggins.

Alan Green (tenor) and I also contributed songs and one of mine was 'Largo al Factotum'. The accompanist was Harold Starling, and he must have been good, because on these occasions, one had only an afternoon rehearsal before the evening's performance.

As I remember it, the concert at Sheringham was distinguished by the fact that several notes were missing from the piano. The orchestra made a successful contribution, but, as far as I can remember, I either did not sing, or I sang unaccompanied. The programme showed 'Songs (Robert Yates) – Selected', in each half.

The Christmas Concert at St Andrew's Hall introduced us to a new local soprano (from King's Lynn) Angela Rose, who contributed to Part I of the *Messiah* and was quite splendid. Frank Weyer was the tenor and Audrey and I completed the cast. Fifteen local choirs sang the choruses and the County Orchestra was led by Leonard Ward. Sidney Twemlow conducted of course, and, in re-examining these old programmes, one must pay tribute to Sidney whose efforts in bringing all these choirs together (fourteen on this occasion), and for the *St Matthew Passion* performance, year after year, were *quite* exceptional. Nothing of this nature occurs in Norfolk today.

6.35 MIDLAND MUSIC CLUB

A magazine programme for
music lovers and concert goers
with
Viola Tunnard and Martin Penny
(piano duets)
Robert Yates (bass-baritone)
Albert Webb (piano)
Introduced by David Franklin
Produced by Reginald Perrin

Chapter 11 - 1958

The Crucifixion (St Mary's Church, Lowestoft) ~ *Carmen* (concert version) (Stuart Hall, Norwich) ~ *Nelson Mass* (Gresham's School, Holt) ~ *St Matthew Passion* (St Andrew's Hall, Norwich) ~ *The Passion of Christ* (St Peter's Church, Strumpshaw) ~ Broadcast (Birmingham) ~ *Elijah* (Barford Church) ~ *Samson* (St Peter's Church, Sheringham) ~ Recital (Cromer Church) ~ *Tom Jones* (concert version) (South Pier Pavilion, Lowestoft) ~ Christmas Concert (St Andrews Hall, Norwich)

Stainer's *Crucifixion* in St Margaret's Church, Lowestoft with the Lowestoft Choral Society was distinguished by daughter Julia, (aged 5) who was in the audience with Audrey, hiccupping in one of my solos.

Elder daughter Elizabeth and Julia were also present at a performance of *Carmen* at the Stuart Hall, Norwich. From the opposite balcony they engaged our attention by dropping toffee papers on the people below. Happily they didn't grow up to be football hooligans. The Stuart Hall was a splendid recital hall, with Suckling Hall linking to form a refreshment area. Later of course, it was to become Cinema City.

Alice Peters had been prominent for some time locally as a soprano soloist, and it was she and David Williams, tenor, who joined Audrey and me in singing in Haydn's *Nelson Mass* at Gresham School. David Williams, as I remember it, was a master at Gresham's.

Eric Greene, tenor was the Evangelist at this year's *St Matthew Passion*. Eric was regarded in top musical circles as being the definitive Evangelist in this work.

Another performance at Strumpshaw Church introduced Jane Manning and Bernard Wesby, tenor. We performed Handel's *The Passion of Christ*, and the Strumpshaw choir was augmented by members of the Barton Turf and District Choral Society. I think it was on this occasion that Charles (the Reverend C.R.B. Coleman) gave us a goat, a present for our singing and for bringing along other soloists. At that time I was singing a Peter Warlock song entitled 'Piggesnie' and the words ran, 'She is so proper and so pure, full steadfast, stable and demure, there is none such, you may be sure, as my sweet Sweeting'. Well, quickly becoming aware of the goat's propensity for taking food in one end and ejecting it at the other, I thought that a slight alteration to the words, substituting 'manure' for 'demure' would be appropriate to the situation so we called her 'Piggy'. We endured a season or so with Piggy, surviving the 6 a.m. efforts at milking, usually ending with her putting a foot in the pail. We also took her for walks, during which it was difficult to restrain her from devouring chunks of any plant she passed. In the end we gave her to a good home.

In June, I was offered another broadcast. I decided to go by train, a decision which was no doubt influenced by a letter from Broadcasting House which read: 'We have managed to book you a room and breakfast for the night of 2nd June at Richmond House Hotel, 22 Harborne Road, Edgbaston, which is within five to six minutes walk from Broadcasting House, at 25/-d'. I shared the recital with

Pamela Beesley, soprano. I sang five songs, only one of which have I ever sung since, which is Roger Quilter's 'Go Lovely Rose'. I will now recount the return train journey. One of the several changes was at Ely. I disembarked and asked the porter from which platform the Norwich connection would leave, and at what time. 'It would leave from Platform 1 at one a.m.' It was then midnight. I decided to have a look at the Cathedral, which, as I remember was quite near. As I approached, all the street lighting and the Cathedral illumination were switched off. I suppose I must have dragged myself back to the station. Anyway, at one a.m. precisely I settled myself into a carriage at Platform 1, which was full of recumbent National Servicemen. Such was the disarray that it was difficult to subdue the feeling of authority that I possessed in this sort of company in the earlier war years. But these thoughts were quickly superseded by the belief that the train was now going back from whence it had come. I aroused one semi-comatose creature to enquire if the train was in fact going back towards March. Yes, it was! I alighted at March, and found refuge for the night in an empty train carriage in a siding, and caught the 6 a.m. train to King's Lynn, from there to Norwich in the company of people commencing their day's work. I cannot remember how I kept Audrey abreast of my adventure, but I suppose I must have 'phoned from a public box because she was at City Station to meet me in my unwashed and unshaven state.

Sidney Twemlow had now decided to form a 'potted opera' group and had enlisted Jane Manning, Bernard Wesby, Peter Hudson and me to present Mozart's *Bastien and Bastienne*, and *The Postbag* by a chap called Esposito, an Italian who for twenty years had been Professor of pianoforte at the Royal Academy of Music, Dublin. This was the start of a series of miniature operas, presented under the auspices of Sidney with Ted Barnell producing. Other works we presented were *Susannah's Secret* by Wolf-Ferarri, *La Serva Padrona* by Pergolesi and *Abu Hassan* by Weber (in which Audrey was involved).

Wherever we went, Sidney would transport us in his car to the places of performance, which were not only in Norfolk, but also sometimes in other counties, and once in London. On one occasion, our destination was the village hall at Hethersett. Having collected us at Costessey, Sidney's selected route was via Ringland Hills. At Easton, there was in those days a ford (now bridged over) just before joining the A45. We had been experiencing heavy weather and the water level in the ford was high. Sidney said, 'How shall I take it Bob – fast or slow?' 'Fast,' I said. We got stuck in the middle. Now from experience in my own car in wet weather I believed the coil needed to dry out, and I estimated that it would take about 15 minutes to dry out. My estimate proved to be correct. Now Sidney was not a man to engage in small talk – he will forgive me for saying that he was almost taciturn in this respect. Imagine our surprise and relief therefore when Sidney, without prompting, recited the whole of 'The Wreck of the Hesperus'. The occasion was also memorable for the fact that Peter Hudson, whilst singing, stuck his foot through a rotten floorboard in the stage, unflinchingly pursuing his aria.

I was engaged to sing Squire Western in a concert performance of *Tom Jones* at the South Pier Pavilion, Lowestoft. The roles of Tom Jones and Sophia were

46

taken by two well-known professionals, John Lawrenson and June Bronhill. I do recall having to help John Lawrenson at rehearsal – he was under-rehearsed due no doubt to pressure of other engagements. I had sung the part of Tom Jones on a previous occasion and managed to prompt him surreptitiously. He was a very pleasant chap and was grateful. Charlotte (Bobby) Pank, with whom we sang so much in those years, sang the part of Honour.

The Lowestoft Choral Society, accompanied by the Millard–Tolhurst Orchestra, was conducted by Claude Richards. Over the years, we were engaged by Claude to contribute to various performances and I can claim to have persuaded a number of soloists with whom we had worked to join us, with Claude, on various Lowestoft platforms.

Handel's oratorio *Samson* which we sang at Sheringham, ought to be sung much more, in my opinion. It contains excellent chorus and solo work. Audrey and I have enjoyed making our contribution to performances of this work on several occasions.

Another *Messiah* at Barford Church, a recital at Cromer Church, and excerpts from *Messiah* at the St Andrew's Hall Christmas Concert, to which Audrey contributed, completed our 1958 musical engagements.

THE LOWESTOFT CHORAL SOCIETY
(AMATEUR)

SOUTH PIER PAVILION

Thursday, 25th September, 1958

at 7.45 p.m.

TOM JONES

by
EDWARD GERMAN
(*by Arrangement with CHAPPELL & Co., Ltd.*)

JOHN LAWRENSON	-	-	-	BASS
JOAN BRAMHALL	-	-	SOPRANO
CHARLOTTE PANK	-	-	SOPRANO
ROBERT YATES	-	-	-	-	BASS

MILLARD-TOLHURST ORCHESTRA
(LEADER : JACK GODDARD)
(ACCOMPANIST : MARIANNE LITTLE)

Conductor : CLAUDE L. RICHARDS

PROGRAMME - - - - *Price SIXPENCE*

Chapter 12 - 1959

Carmen (concert version) (Dereham Memorial Hall) ~ Recital (Loddon Methodist Church) Fauré's *Requiem* (Gresham's School, Holt) ~ *Olivet to Calvary* (St Margaret's Church, Lowestoft) ~ *Messiah* (Norton Church) ~ *Bastien and Bastienne* (Assembly House, Norwich) ~ *The Postbag* (Assembly House, Norwich) ~ *Messiah* (Cromer Church) ~ Concert (Assembly House, Norwich) ~ *Messiah* (Loddon Methodist, Church) ~ Concert (Sir John Leman School, Beccles) ~ *Christmas Oratorio* (Town Hall, Great Yarmouth) ~ *Fantasia on Christmas Carols* (Christmas Concert, St Andrew's Hall, Norwich) ~ Christmas Concert (Chaucer Institute, Bungay)

Another *Carmen* at Dereham. How we must have flogged Bizet's masterpiece in these years.

A recital at Loddon Methodist Church included three arias from Handel's *Samson*, two bass and one contralto. Audrey also sang one of Dvorak's Biblical Songs. The programme shows that our accompanist was Mrs M.A. Farey. (Programme compilers in these days still seemed reluctant to use Christian names.) If my memory serves me correctly, Mrs Farey was the wife of the then recently retired Chief Superintendent Farey of the Norfolk Police. This must be correct, because surely only a musical association could have resulted in our being asked to tea at their house.

I sang in a Fauré's *Requiem* at Gresham's School with Jane Manning, who was now emerging as a soloist in the county. In fact Audrey and I were to sing a great deal with Jane before and after she studied at the Royal Academy, until she decided to take up singing as a career. At her wedding to Anthony Payne, then music critic for *The Daily Telegraph* I think, and now, one of Britain's leading composers, Jane's father Gerald asked me to speak instead of him. I think he was losing his nerve for public singing and speaking. I was proud to undertake this privilege. Tony, as well as Jane, has of course gone on to greater fame, having pieced together the various writings left by Elgar of what was to have been his Third Symphony to produce, through his own musical invention, a Third Symphony indistinguishable in character from Elgar's own work, and to gain the approbation of Elgar's family.

Olivet to Calvary at Lowestoft gives me the opportunity of mentioning Cyril Mitchell, organist, an extremely capable musician, who accompanied me on this and several other occasions.

A *Messiah* at Norton Parish church with the Beccles Choral Society is memorable for the fact that the organist was unable to accomplish the speed of accompaniment required for 'Why do the Nations', resulting in my proceeding for most of the aria unaccompanied. In his defence, it must be said that the *Messiah* is written for orchestra and voices, and the piano and organ accompaniment versions are brutal, requiring from the accompanist, either much practice to maintain speeds, or a little 'juggling'. Performances of this nature

48

usually took place in the evening, after an afternoon rehearsal. It might have been that on this occasion there was no rehearsal because, like every other choral society, *Messiah* was in their repertoire, as it was in ours.

Now, in foraging my 1959 file, I have found a programme of Mozart's *Bastien and Bastienne* and *The Postbag*, both referred to earlier. The performance was at the Assembly House and the cast list contains the names of those singers recorded in my earlier reference to this Group. (How different a meaning the title 'Group' now conveys). In this year's folder, I find notice of *Abu Hassan* and *Susannah's Secret* being performed at the Assembly House in November.

Later on, we were to take these small operas, and others, to Lady Delia Peel's residence, Barton Turf Hall. On one such occasion, Lady Delia invited me to a take a glass of sherry with her in her drawing room, where she told me that Horatio Nelson had left that room to take up his first appointment with the Admiralty. On another occasion, when Audrey was also singing, she presented me with a brace of woodcocks!

A *Messiah* at Cromer included Anne Pashley as soprano soloist (I think that by this time she had become a member of Welsh Opera). David Holman, tenor, was also a professional.

A concert at the Assembly House included a group of songs from both Jane Manning and myself, and those two ubiquitous duets for soprano and baritone from Mozarts *The Magic Flute* and *Don Giovanni*. We were accompanied by Barbara Coyle who also accompanied Francesca Brennan ('cello). Further contributions were by Kenneth Dobson (pianoforte) and Michael McKenna, oboist. Michael was the son of John McKenna previously referred to. Barbara Coyle was Jane's music mistress at Norwich High School, and Jane tells me that Barbara encouraged her to take up singing.

The programme of the Christmas Concert at St Andrew's Hall, conducted as ever by Sidney Twemlow, reveals that the soloists were Jane Manning, Audrey Yates, Bernard Wesby and Laurence Mallyon. Laurence was a full bass and broadcast from Birmingham, at least once to my knowledge, a programme of negro spirituals, to which his voice was admirably suited. Organ continuo was by Geoffrey Laycock, piano continuo by Bernard Burrell, with the orchestra led by Harry Thornton, all memorable names.

The concert with the Bungay Choral Society, included contributions by the choir and myself and, in the second half, Vaughan Williams' *Fantasia on Christmas Carols*.

We sang another *Messiah* at Loddon, with Angela Dugdale singing the soprano solos. Angela was to become quite famous locally for pioneering and conducting the Broadland Singers for thirty or more years.

Audrey and I contributed to a concert with the Beccles Choral Society. Our contributions were groups of songs in addition to which I sang the baritone solos in Stanford's *Songs of the Sea*. Reginald Firth, who conducted was a very gentle man. He and his wife Mary (previously mentioned and on this occasion playing piano) were a splendid combination and there is no doubt that they made memorable contributions to the Beccles musical scene. Moreover, Mary conducted massed Townswomen's Guild choirs in many prestigious venues throughout Norfolk.

Christmas Oratorio (Parts 1 & II) at Yarmouth was of special interest because we (The Great Yarmouth Musical Society and soloists) were accompanied by a string quartet, and not by full orchestra. We enjoyed it tremendously. Audrey and I also sang a group of songs, accompanied by Harold Starling, upon whose excellence I have previously remarked, and I joined the choir by singing the baritone solos in Vaughan Williams' *Fantasia on Christmas Carols*. Worthy of note is that the tenor on this occasion was Walter Shackleton, noted Cathedral singer, and father of Margaret Johnson and Sylvia Shackleton, both of whom, together with their husbands, Dennis Johnson and David Watering respectively, were to feature in our future music-making.

The concert hall within the Town Hall was a splendid venue for performances by the Musical Societies, and I feel sad that it is no longer used for this purpose.

I mentioned our Bond mini-car earlier. What I didn't mentioned is that on more than one homeward journey, we would run out of petrol and have to push the car home, not only in the Bond, but with other vintage conveyances which we humoured with just enough petrol (we would think) for the return journey. Propelling the Bond without petrol was easy. We were so near the ground that we could paddle it with a stick, which we carried for that purpose.

Perhaps I ought to tell you a little more about the Bond, since, like all our cars, it was heavily involved in our musical activities. The windscreen was opaque at night, so that you had to stick your head out at the side, or elevate yourself from the driving seat to peer over the top (on a dry night with the hood down). On one occasion, I recall that somewhere near Trowse, and heading either for Beccles or Lowestoft, the car lighting system became recalcitrant. You could either have your headlights on, or your rear lights, not both at the same time. Audrey solved the matter by shining a torch through the lining of a red coat to give us a rear light. In spite of this and other car-travelling vicissitudes, with the help variously of the A.A., other motorists or God, we seem to have been successful in meeting our musical obligations.

Chapter 13 - 1960

Concert (Holt) ~ Music for Christmas (Diss Parish Church) ~ *St Matthew Passion* (St Andrew's, Norwich) Concert (Grammar School Hall, Lowestoft) *Israel in Egypt* (St Mary's Baptist Church, Norwich) ~ *Susannah's Secret* (Assembly House, Norwich) ~ Concert (Acle) ~ *Susannah's Secret* (White Horse Inn, Brundall) ~ *The Creation* (Trinity Methodist Church, Dereham, and Swanton Morley Parish Church) ~ Concert (North Walsham) ~ Christmas Concert and *Messiah* (St Andrew's Hall, Norwich)

I have said that it would be tedious to mention every name of those musicians who were involved in our many concerts. I now find it difficult to catalogue these events without quoting some of the names of those who shared these experiences, and without whose excellence we could not have performed. I shall therefore have to risk tedium of repetition when quoting them.

Let me therefore say that out Holt performance was in the company of the Holt Choral Society, two other soloists Dorothy Osbourne and David Williams, and that the instrumentalists were Michael Butcher, Cecil Brennan (flutes), George Milnes (viola), Barry Wright and Frank Pond ('cellos), Norman Cutting (organ), conductor Michael Allard.

The annual *St Matthew Passion* included Eric Greene as the Evangelist once again. Audrey, Jane Manning, Bernard Wesby, Wilfred Copestake and myself were all local singers. Leaders of the orchestra were Harry Thornton and Margaret Bidwell (later Margaret Dye). The piano continuo was by Stephen Wilkinson, and the organ continuo by Geoffrey Laycock. Fourteen choirs and two orchestras were involved. Stephen Wilkinson became the renowned conductor of the BBC Northern Singers.

I joined with the Lowestoft Choral Society, conducted by Claude Richards, to sing Stanford Robinson's *Plantation Songs*. Additionally, I presented two groups of songs, and when I say that one of the groups included Rossini's 'Largo al factotum' you will appreciate the excellence of the piano accompanist, Marianne Little, with whom I had only an afternoon rehearsal. Marianne was a delightful lady, later to become Marianne Long. How she must have suffered from observations on this titular metamorphosis!

Israel in Egypt at St Mary's Baptist Church, Norwich, was performed jointly by the the Sheringham and Cromer Choral Society and the St Mary's Choir, conducted by Norman Cutting, with Cyril Pearse at the organ. These two choirs shared many a concert, reciprocally at Cromer Church and St Mary's Baptist Church, Norman and Cyril being the resident maestros at these establishments. Audrey sang the contralto solos and Richard White the tenor solos. This was the first of many occasions that we shared the platform with Richard.

We presented *Susannah's Secret* and *Abu Hassan* at the Assembly House and *Susannah's Secret* again in November at The White Horse Inn, Brundall. The Assembly House performance was accompanied by Eileen Bidwell, and the

PROGRAMME

ABU HASSAN	-	-	-	-	WEBER		

Abu Hassan, favourite of the Caliph - - PETER HUDSON

Fatima, his wife - - - - - - JANE MANNING

Omar, a banker - - - - - LAWRENCE MALLYON

Mesrur - - - - - - EDWARD BARNELL

Zemrud - - - - - - - AUDREY YATES

The Caliph - - - - - WILLIAM RUDDERHAM

Zobeide - - - - - - LOUISE RUDDEN

Scene—A room in Abu Hassan's house in Baghdad

Abu Hassan and his wife are, as usual, insolvent. The imposture by which they get themselves out of their difficulties earns by its impudence the Caliph's amused forgiveness and disgraces their principal creditor by revealing him in compromising circumstances.

INTERVAL OF
FIFTEEN MINUTES

SUSANNA'S SECRET		ERMANNO WOLF-FERRARI

Count Gil - - - - - - - ROBERT YATES

The Countess Susanna - - - CHARLOTTE PANK

Sante, a servant - - - - EDWARD BARNELL

Scene—The house of Count Gil in Piedmont

Count Gil has been married to the Countess Susanna for just a month. He detests the habit of smoking. His wife, who cannot resist it, indulges herself, with the complicity of Sante, in secret. The smell of smoke about the house, and even in Susanna's clothes, makes the Count draw a wrong conclusion and Susanna's prevarications make the misunderstanding worse. When at last the Count discovers the truth his relief is such that he gladly pardons Susanna and agrees in future to join her in smoking.

Stage Manager - William Rudderham

Lighting by Peter Hollingham

Norfolk Opera Group at the Assembly House 1960

Brundall performance by Gladys King. Gladys King also accompanied Michael McKenna, oboe and David Watering, clarinet, in items by Handel and Weber. Gladys was John McKenna's sister-in-law; Michael was his son. John's wife sang a splendid contralto, making this family musically notable. The programme for the Acle concert lists 'Mr and Mrs Robert Yates' as having rendered vocal solos. I don't know what we sang, but we were accompanied by a young pianist, Gillian Osborne, who was emerging as a gifted performer. The Brundall Orchestra also performed under the baton of Miss L. Ainsworth.

The Creation by Haydn at Dereham and Swanton Morley, was accompanied by David Kett and conducted by Edwin Kennedy. As I write this, the ubiquitous David is still playing and conducting throughout the county and many is the occasion before and since this year of 1960 that we have shared performances. David lived and still lives in Thorpe St Andrew, and once told me that when he was a boy, he would listen to me singing in a house nearby. What fortitude! The house in question must have been that of my pianist at that time.

The concert at North Walsham, was presented by the combined choirs of North Walsham and Holt Choral Societies, conducted by John Boyce and Geoffrey Laycock. Audrey and I contributed Bach arias, with obligatos by Joy Marflitt, violin, and John McKenna, oboe.

The Christmas Concert at St Andrew's Hall (conductor Sidney Twemlow, as ever) involved fourteen choirs and two orchestras, and it is interesting to note that our old friend the Reverend Charles Coleman, is listed once again as one of the conductors responsible for training choirs prior to their assembly en masse on the day of performance. Other conductors with whom we were associated in other musical venues, were Mrs R Alborough, Bernard Burrell, Eric Balls, Elsie Edmunds, Sylvia Foxwell, Jack Gibson, Edwin Kennedy, Michael Sanders, and Leonard Ward. Soloists on this occasion, when *Messiah* Part 1 formed the first part of the programme, were Beryl Mann, soprano, Bernard Wesby, tenor, and Audrey and myself.

Chapter 14 - 1961

Songs of the Fleet & other songs (Sir John Leman School, Beccles) ~
St Matthew Passion (St Andrews Hall, Norwich) ~ Brahm's *Requiem*
(Congregational Church, Bungay) ~ Concert (Townswomen's Guilds,
Town Hall, Great Yarmouth) ~ Recital (Loddon Methodist Church) ~
The Bartered Bride (concert version) (Grammar School Hall, Lowestoft)
~ Recital (Blofield Church) ~ *Creation* (Cromer Church) ~ Concert
(Stuart Hall, Norwich) ~ *Creation* (St Mary's Baptist Church, Norwich)
~ Concert (Inc. *Plantation Songs*) (Town Hall, Great Yarmouth) ~
Acis and Galatea (Sir John Leman School, Beccles) ~ Christmas Concert
(Norwich Union) (Assembly House, Norwich)

It seems to have been another busy year, and with the repetition of so many
familiar works, I shall try to limit myself to mentioning performers whom I
haven't mentioned before, and recounting any episode, which might be of
interest to the reader.

The Beccles concert included songs from both Audrey and myself and
Stanford's *Songs of the Fleet* in which I added my solo efforts to those of the
Beccles Choral Society, augmented on this occasion by tenors of Norwich
Singers. *Songs of the Fleet* is a stirring maritime composition, a sequel to *Songs of
the Sea*, in which I had joined the Beccles choir on an earlier occasion.

St Matthew Passion with Eric Greene once more. New faces were Peter
Currell, tenor and George James, bass. Hilary Clouting led one of the two
orchestras (more of her in later reminiscences). This year the event took place at
the Cathedral. The three hundred odd choristers were packed into the chancel
and choir stalls, rank after rank. The orchestra had settled itself. There was no
Eric Greene. It was known that he was staying at The Maid's Head, so an urgent
expedition to that establishment was made. I understand that Eric was either
asleep or resting in the belief that the performance commenced at 8 p.m. not
7.30 p.m. He arrived in a very few minutes. Later we learned, when enjoying
supper with him and Jane Manning, that he was a connoisseur of good wines.
Could it be that this had some relevance to his relaxed approach to the
performance? Jane, it should be recorded, had been studying with Eric Greene at
the Royal Academy of Music from 1956–1960. The press critic on these
auspicious occasions had always been the Reverend Basil Maine and I think that
his critique reflected a fair judgement of the performances.

In Brahms' *Requiem* with the Bungay Choral Society, I was again with Jane
Manning. Programmes on one sheet of paper cost 3d, which I hope didn't reflect
the quality of the performance.

The East Anglian Federation of Townswomen's Guilds engaged Audrey and
myself as soloists for their concert at Yarmouth Town Hall. Conducted by Mary
Firth, the piano accompanist was John Hammond. The choir sangVaughan
Williams' *Folk Songs of the Four Seasons*. John Hammond played some Chopin
and Dohnanyi. Amongst the very demanding songs that I had chosen was

PROGRAMME

PART I

THE QUEEN

Chorus

"IN WINDSOR FOREST"

A Cantata for Mixed Voices

Music adapted from the Opera "Sir John in Love" by Ralph Vaughan Williams

(I)   The Conspiracy ("*Sigh no more Ladies*") Women's voices

(II) The Drinking Song ("*Back and Side go Bare*") Men's voices

(III) Falstaff and the Fairies ("*Round about in a fair ring-a*")

(IV) Wedding Chorus ("*See the Chariot at Hand*")

(V)   Epilogue ("*Whether Men do laugh or weep*")

AUDREY YATES   *Contralto*

Verdant Meadows	*Handel*
The Lovers Strategy	*Brahms*
Invocation	*Franz*

ROBERT YATES   *Baritone*

The Jolly Beggar   ....   *Victor Hely Hutchinson*

When a maiden takes your fancy from Il Seraglio   *Mozart*

Song of the Flea   ....   *Moussorgsky*

INTERVAL

Coffee will be served in the School Dining Hall

PART II

AUDREY YATES   *Contralto*

Kilarney	...... *Balfe*
Funny Fellow	*Michael Head*

Chorus   **"SONGS OF THE FLEET"**

for Baritone Solo and Chorus set to music by Charles V. Stanford, Op. 117

(I)   Sailing at Dawn

(II)   The Song of the Sou' Wester

(III) The Middle Watch

(IV)   The Little Admiral

(V)   Fare Well

The Society wishes to express appreciation to the Norwich Singers (tenors) who are kindly assisting in this performance.

Concert at Beccles, 1951

55

Schubert's 'The Erl King'. Need I say more about the accomplishments of the pianist? Fifteen Guild Choirs contributed to the concert, and Mary Firth conducted them.

Two new names appear in the programme for 'Music for a Sunday Evening' at Loddon Methodist Church, those of Nigel Hamilton, pianoforte, and, in addition to Mrs Farey again, Mr F. Clemence, accompanying either Audrey or myself or Andrew Barnell playing bassoon. Andrew was later to join the Birmingham Symphony Orchestra.

The Lowestoft Choral Society sang Brahms' *Song of Destiny*, and Jane Manning and I, together with Edgar Thomas, tenor, joined them in a concert version of *The Bartered Bride*. I think it must have been on this occasion that on the return journey I missed the Norwich route where the road divided (now a roundabout) and we found ourselves in Yarmouth. The reason was quite an innocent one, although others to whom I have related the incident have raised an eyebrow. The fact is that Jane is a good talker, always interesting, in which circumstances the car would seem to make its own decisions.

With *Creation* at Cromer, Richard White sang tenor, consolidating a long association with him, both as a tenor and later as a producer. I well remember Richard, apropos these early associations, saying that as a boy, he had attended performances in which Audrey and I were involved. It has to be said here that Audrey must have been very young at the time.

The concert at the Stuart Hall, Norwich, conducted by Hugh Skeens included songs from other contributors and me of which I have little memory. It also included excerpts from Vaughan Williams' *Serenade to Music* (Robert Yates, Bernard Wesby, Grace Lee) and the Waltz scene and Finale to Act 3 of Gounod's *Faust* (Mephistopheles, Robert Yates, Faust, Bernard Wesby, Seibel, Marjorie Riach, Marguerite Gladys Abel.) Marjorie Riach is also listed as accompanist. Could it have been that she accompanied me in 'Largo al Factotum'? Or did I take my own accompanist, and if so, why was he or she not listed? One failure of programmes in those days seems to have been this appalling omission of the singer's accompanist's name.

Creation at St Mary's Baptist Church is another instance of a return match after playing at Cromer; although this time, the Sheringham and Cromer Choral Society were joined by the Catton Choral Society, Great Yarmouth Musical Society and St Mary's Choir.

The Yarmouth concert is interesting. It includes a work called *The Rhyming Shipman* by Thomas B. Pitfield (b. 1903), 'a whimsical cantata for baritone solo and chorus'. I can remember absolutely nothing about this. They seem to have worked me pretty hard, because I also sang six songs, and sang the baritone solos in Stanford Robinson's *Plantation Songs*.

Acis and Galatea at Beccles was conducted by Reginald Firth, with a small ensemble so often present on these occasions, led by Colin Clouting, with Jack Wilde, violin, George Milnes, viola, John Martin, 'cello. The choir also performed a work by Brahms, the English title of which is 'Marie'.

I have spoken of Lesli Kurl before. I was with him again at Blofield Parish Church, together with Francesca Brennan ('cello) Dudley Brennan (pianoforte) and Gillian Osborne, solo pianist, and accompanist. Once again, my mind boggles at the virtuosity of pianists such as Gillian who are able to meet the physical requirements of the accompaniment to 'The Erl King', which I performed on this occasion.

The Christmas concert with the Norwich Union Choral Society ended our year's performances. Four of us, Beryl Mann, Bernard Wesby, Audrey and myself, were involved as soloists in the *Messiah* Part 1, and we rendered a variety of quartets in the second half.

This is not quite all of my public performances in 1961, because it was in this year that I became the first presenter of advertisements for Anglia Television. Although not musical contributions, they came about through my musical connections in this fashion. Chris Peal was a member of the staff of Anglia Television, which had taken up residence in the old Agricultural Hall in Norwich in 1960. We had recently persuaded him to join the chorus of the Dereham Operatic Society. He was a splendid-looking man, though not musically outstanding. Chris's major accomplishments lay in other fields (he was a good tennis player and had a marvellous pewter collection) but I think that at that time his pursuit of Sheila Mellonie (already in the society and later to become his wife) lessened the difficulty of our persuasion.

I am not certain what methods were employed in advertising by Anglia Television in 1960 – perhaps representatives of the firms advertising were used - but in 1961 they were out to appoint their own presenter. Chris (as sales executive) came to my office one day, saying that in his quest for a suitable candidate he had so far been unsuccessful – would I audition? I agreed, and in due course presented myself to Studio 4, a small room, in the premises previously known as the Agricultural Hall, but now extensively adapted to become the headquarters of Anglia Television. Upon my arrival this room became crowded with people, each with his own brief, one presenting me with a script, another arranging me in my chair, others seemingly discussing deep subjects entirely removed from the matter in hand, but suddenly pouncing on the script and revising it, and, when all this was settled, the clapper-boy (man actually) would clap his board. 'Take number One' was under way. I can't remember whether there was 'Take No. Two,' or Three or Four but the boss man (I forget his title) gave me the thumbs up. During the year I advertised Scotch Brand tape for Jarrolds, turkeys for the Le Grys Bros. of Ubbeston, near Halesworth, something (I know not what) for Leeder and Griffiths Ltd. of Newmarket, Professor Marchal seed wheat for Sinclair's of Boston and finally (I'll explain the 'finally' later) accommodation at the Carlton Hotel, Great Yarmouth. This assignment was to have been carried out by Bruce Forsyth who was performing in Yarmouth, but apparently his contract precluded him from taking other paid engagements, so Anglia's resident presenter, yours truly, was asked to take over. Let me just give you some detail of the assignment as listed on my brief:

'Treatment – Open on fascia of Hotel building to include the Carlton's name. Pan down to doorway where presenter is leaving the hotel. Conversation between

Hotel Host and presenter:
'Goodbye Mr Yates'.
Mr Yates: 'Goodbye, and thank you for a wonderful time. By the way, what happens here in the winter?'
Host: 'We have dinner dances and private banquets.' Mr Yates: 'My word, well, if you plan a night out or a really special weekend there's nowhere better than the Carlton Hotel, Yarmouth.' – ½ second silent.

This may sound straightforward, but we took all morning, satisfaction only reached after the microphone had been placed in a dozen different places. Holiday crowds were enjoying it. Finally we received the thumbs up, but considerably more than ½ second's silence must have been required because at least two seconds after the thumbs up the host said to me, 'Come and have a pink gin.' We were consummating that activity when the clapper-boy (man) arrived and said to me 'You spoke.' Well, I couldn't very well say, 'I didn't, it was him,' could I? Nevertheless it necessitated a further 'take'. I was never asked again. It had been an interesting interlude and money received from the presenting had enabled me to buy a new jacket, the first one having to be exchanged because the pattern conflicted with the television cameras, but its replacement served me for many more occasions than the television commercials for which it was bought. My last assignment reads:

Fees for one Television Commercial TV 266	
For recording	£7. 7. 0
First repeat	£7. 7. 0
17 repeats at 14/9d	£12. 10. 9
	£27. 4. 9

This may look trivial today, but it was useful money then.

THE SHERINGHAM & CROMER CHORAL SOCIETY

President : *The Revd. KEITH WARNER, B.A.*

With St. Mary's Choir, Norwich and singers from North Walsham.

ELIJAH

BY

FELIX MENDELSSOHN BARTHOLDY

IN

CROMER PARISH CHURCH
Tuesday, 31st July, 1962

At 7-45 p.m.

Soloists :

SUSANNAH MYLECHREEST	Soprano
AUDREY YATES -	Contralto
PHILIP LANGRIDGE -	Tenor
ROBERT YATES -	Bass

Leader of the Orchestra : SYDNEY GOULD

Organist : CYRIL PEARCE, L.R.A.M., A.R.C.M.

Conductor : NORMAN A. CUTTING, B.MUS., F.R.C.O., A.R.C.M.

PROGRAMME ONE SHILLING

59

Chapter 15 - 1962

Iolanthe (concert version) (South Pier Pavilion, Lowestoft) ~ Gilbert & Sullivan excerpts (Dereham Memorial Hall and Assembly House, Norwich) ~ *St John Passion* (St Nicholas Chapel, King's Lynn) ~ *Elijah* (Cromer Church) ~ *Messiah* (Philharmonic) (St Andrew's Hall, Norwich) Wedding (John & Marjorie Standley, Wymondham Abbey) ~ Concert (The Church of St George, Samford Brett) ~ Concert (Blofield Church) ~ Concert (inc. *Hiawatha's Departure*, Stuart Hall, Norwich) ~ *Songs of the Fleet* (Tacket Street) *The Bartered Bride* (concert version) (Congregational Church, Ipswich) ~ Christmas Concert (inc. *The Peasant Cantata*) (St Edmund's Hall, Southwold)

I was becoming an entrepreneur for Claude Richards, conductor of the Lowestoft Choral Society. For their performances of a concert version of *Iolanthe*, I recruited Alec Forbes-Wright as Lord Chancellor, Richard White as Earl Tolloller, Barry Saull as Private Willis, Michael Drake as Strephon, Anne Youngman as Celia and Bridget Grief as Lelia. Jane Manning, whom I had recruited earlier, sang the part of Phyllis, whilst Audrey was Queen of the Fairies, and I was Lord Mountararat. Marianne Long, pianist, was then, as ever, with the Augmented Millard-Tolhurst Orchestra led by Jack Goddard.

There were also some new names in a concert of excerpts from the two Gilbert & Sullivan operas, *The Yeomen of the Guard* and *The Mikado* performed at the Memorial Hall, Dereham by the Elmham and District Choral Society. (They had not yet changed their name to the Mid-Norfolk Singers). Edwin Kennedy was conducting and David Kett accompanying at the piano. Names of new soloists were Mary Brown, Tom Ashcroft, Hilton Tait and Ruby Eastell.

This concert was repeated at the Assembly House the following week.

Audrey sang in Bach's *St John Passion* at St Nicholas Chapel, King's Lynn. The bass role was sung by George James, who had recently moved to Norwich. George was an excellent bass, an ex-professional, and now a member of the Cathedral choir. Jane Manning and Bernard Wesby were soprano and tenor respectively.

The performance of *Elijah* at Cromer is significant in that the tenor role was taken by Philip Langridge, well known professional. The soprano was Susannah Mylechreest. I cannot recall anything about her musical pedigree.

Audrey's big moment came when she was asked by the Norwich Philharmonic Society to sing the contralto arias in a performance of Handel's *Messiah*, parts 1 & II, in the distinguished company of three top-ranking professionals, Heather Harper, soprano, Gerald English, tenor and Roger Stalman, bass. The conductor was Antony Hopkins. Press reports were most complimentary.

Since Audrey and I were married in Wymondham Abbey, I think it is in order to mention that Audrey returned there to sing on the occasion of a relative's wedding, in May of this year.

NORWICH SINGER IN 'MESSIAH' TOMORROW

OF ALL THE TIMES the Norwich singer Mrs. Audrey Yates has sung in the "Messiah," none has held a more exciting prospect than her engagement for this Good Friday.

She has been chosen to take the contralto part in the Norwich Philharmonic Society performance of Parts 2 and 3 of the oratorio at St. Andrew's Hall, conducted this year by the popular broadcaster, Antony Hopkins. Beside her will be soloists with national reputations, Heather Harper (soprano), Gerald English (tenor) and Roger Stalman (bass).

Most Widely Known

With the exception of Miss Virginia Hastings, who, although of Norfolk origin, had been studying in Italy when she appeared two years ago, it will be the first time a local singer has been engaged for many years. The contralto has mostly been a student from one of the main musical colleges.

For years, Mrs. Yates and her husband, the bass Robert Yates, have been the most widely known singers in Norfolk. They have had literally hundreds of engagements in oratorio, opera and concerts throughout the county, many of them for charity.

Practically all their leisure is taken up with their joint hobby. " It would not be any exaggeration to say that almost every evening is devoted to music," Mr. Yates told a reporter. " because we are always rehearsing even when we are at home,"

Often they have several engagements in a week.

Mr. Yates began singing in Thorpe St. Andrew Parish Church choir, in which he was boy soloist at the age of 12, and his wife appeared in

Mrs. Audrey Yates, of West End, Old Costessey, who is one of the principals in the Good Friday performance of the "Messiah" at St. Andrew's Hall, Norwich.

By courtesy of Eastern Counties Newspapers

I have previously mentioned our friend the Reverend Charles Coleman. He moved to Somerset to become priest at The Church of St George at Sampford Brett. We visited him and his wife Evelyn many times when the children were young. I have a programme of an occasion in August of this year when Audrey and I sang first at an Evensong on Sunday, and then at a 'Musical Evening at the Rectory' on the Monday. This element of our visits was repeated more than once, and introduced us to some charming local musicians. A couple of incidents not related to our musical activities were that on one visit Julia, immediately upon arrival, bashed a tennis ball through a window. Audrey and I had developed DIY skills, which enabled me to replace it quickly. On another occasion Elizabeth, riding for the first time, was put astride a horse owned by Charles and Evelyn and used by their daughter. It bolted at full gallop on to the main Taunton Road, and finally deposited Lizzie there. Commandeering the first vehicle to appear, we followed. 'Follow that horse,' I commanded. Young bones are resilient, and she was unhurt.

'A concert of Vocal and Instrumental Music' was held at Blofield Parish Church in September. The instrumentalists were Francesca Brennan, 'cello, and Dudley Brennan, pianoforte, a man and wife team of exceptional quality. Audrey sang songs, I sang an aria from Handel's *Samson*, but the evening was most notable for me because of my performing *Songs of the Apocalypse*, specially written by none other than Lesli Kurl. (How dare I have said such things about him earlier in this document?) It was the first performance of this work. Lesli accompanied me at the piano, but the instrumentalists were accompanied by Reginald Bolton, whom we knew for his performances as conductor of Catton Choral Society and organist in other church concerts. I still have the *Songs of the Apocalypse* and must look at them again sometime.

The concert at the Stuart Hall was again with the St. Cecilia Chorus and Orchestra. The evening included a performance of *Hiawatha's Departure* which is a setting of the final part of Longfellow's colourful poem. Other soloists were Barbara Land, Frank Weyer and Gladys Abel.

Gordon Hawkins was Bursar at the Royal Naval College at Holbrook. A performance at Tacket Street Congregational Church, Ipswich, was the first of several to which Audrey and I contributed, at Gordon's invitation. He and his wife were extremely pleasant, and I recall many an afternoon cup of tea at their house before proceeding to Ipswich. On this occasion, the items performed were Stanford's *Songs of the Fleet* and a concert version of the *The Bartered Bride*.

The Christmas concert by the Southwold Choral Society and the Southwold Orchestral Society included Bach's *Peasant Cantata*. Other soloists were Dora Fox, contralto and Mary Brown, soprano. Dora Fox also conducted the choir and orchestra in works for the choir, *In Windsor Forest* by Vaughan Williams and 'Cowboy Carol' arranged by Malcolm Sargent. Once again, I am amazed to find that my contributions of songs included Rossini's 'Largo al Factotum' to the piano accompaniment of Grenville Smith. The piano accompaniment calls for much dexterity, and the inference is that the several pianists with whom I have performed this aria must have been extremely skilful to have performed after one rehearsal. 'Tis true, the pianist would have had prior notice, since one's choice of songs had to be submitted beforehand for the programme printing.

In this year, Audrey and I decided to form an opera company. The reader will have deduced from the preceding page that for some years our musical contributions had been with Norfolk and Suffolk Choral Societies of which we were not members, but merely visiting soloists. All of these occasions were memorable, but we now felt a desire to perform opera again, as we had done earlier. The Norfolk and Norwich Amateur Operatic Company were performing light opera and musicals and we had no wish to compete in that field. There seemed to be scope for a company producing operatic works that were not travelled by visiting professional companies, and would otherwise seldom or never be seen in Norfolk. With the encouragement of Jane Manning, we gathered together twenty singers who owed no allegiance to other societies and formed The Norfolk Opera Players. We started modestly with ballad opera in the shape of *The Beggar's Opera*, and were rehearsing this in 1962, in preparation for its performance in 1963.

Chapter 16 - 1963

Hugh Gaitskell's Memorial Service (St Peter Mancroft, Norwich) ~
Samson (St Andrew's Church, Norwich) ~ Bach's *Magnificat* and
Haydn's *Mass in B flat* (Beccles Church) ~ Gilbert & Sullivan excerpts
(Dereham Memorial Hall) *Messiah* (St Albans Church, Norwich) ~
St Matthew Passion (Tacket Street Congregational Church, Ipswich) ~
Merrie England (concert version) (St Andrew's Hall, Norwich) ~
H.M.S. Pinafore (concert version) (Aylsham Evening Institute.) ~
The Beggar's Opera (Cromer Pier Pavilion) ~ *St Paul* (Cromer Church)
Hiawatha's Wedding Feast & Departure (South Pier Pavilion, Lowestoft)
~ *The Beggar's Opera* (Maddermarket Theatre, Norwich) ~ Recital
(Wymondham Abbey) ~ *The Mikado* (concert version) (Assembly House,
Norwich) ~ *Christmas Oratorio* (King's Lynn Technical College) ~
Gondoliers (concert version) (South Pier Pavilion, Lowestoft)

In January, I was privileged to sing at a memorial service to Hugh Gaitskell, contributing a rendition of Hymn No.293, 'Who would true valour see'.

Samson evoked this introductory statement from the Press critic: 'Handel's oratorio *Samson* can hardly have been performed in Norwich within living memory, until last night... when Catton Choral Society presented it at St Andrew's Church.' As stated earlier, I am surprised and disappointed that this oratorio is not performed more frequently in Norfolk, containing as it does such excellent work for soloists, chorus and orchestra. The conductor was George James, whose fine bass singing I have previously commended. I can't recall which orchestra it was, probably ad hoc, although the press critique reads: 'The orchestra was strengthened by members of Norwich Philharmonic Society.'

I have a Press photograph of choir, orchestra and soloists at the afternoon rehearsal of Bach's *Magnificat* and Haydn's *Mass in B flat*, at Beccles super-imposed with the statement: 'Our music critic says this was one of the finest concerts given by the society.' I am not disposed to challenge this. Individual contributors were Beryl Mann, soprano, Brian Burrows, tenor, (now I believe a London-based professional) Audrey and myself, John Hammond, organ, Mary Firth, pianist, leader of orchestra Colin Clouting, conductor, Reginald Firth.

This might be the right time to mention Roland Reynolds, secretary to the Beccles Choral Society. Like all secretaries he worked like a beaver, present at every aspect of rehearsal and performance, moving from place to place, as I seem to recollect, with the speed and style of Basil Fawlty. He and his wife Winifred both sang in the choir. Winifred (known to everyone as 'Win') always used a very pale make-up, making her rather conspicuous amongst the other more pinkish (and even rubicund when singing) choristers. Waiting for our turn to rehearse (soloists were always the last on these occasions) and sitting in the church pews, Beryl remarked 'I see Win has been at the old flour bag again.' It was not until then that we noticed a microphone attached to the next pew.

Concert in Beccles Church, 1963

The Elmham & District Choral Society still retained that name in this year. We sang excerpts from *The Pirates of Penzance* and *Iolanthe* with them in Dereham Memorial Hall. Quite a few members of the Society were included in the casting.

A *Messiah*, at St Alban's Church, Norwich, featured Olive McKenna as contralto soloist. I have paid tribute to her earlier, remember? The soprano was Valerie Walker and the tenor Albert Pye, conductor George James.

Gordon Hawkins recruited Audrey and me to sing in a *St Matthew Passion* at Ipswich. The other soloists were, I think, either local amateurs or professionals.

Fifteen ladies' choirs gathered in St Andrew's Hall for a concert performance of Edward German's *Merrie England*. They were of course, choirs of the East Anglia Federation of Townswomen's Guilds, conducted by Marty Firth and accompanied at the piano by John Hammond. Audrey and I were there, as also were Charlotte Pank, Peter Hudson, George Allison, Michael Drake, Donald MacKenzie and Wallace Stoatley. At the afternoon rehearsal, one of the ladies fainted. She was singing from the top of the then deeply-tiered stage. Singing the role of The Earl of Essex, how could I not have dashed up to carry her down? I did.

Jane Manning had by this time completed her training at the Royal Academy and become a music teacher at Aylsham Secondary Modern School. During her time there she also founded the Aylsham Choral Society. She conducted them in a concert performance of *H.M.S. Pinafore*. Other soloists were Leslie and Gladys Mallyon, Doris Walmsley, Harry Bowen, Peter Meaney and, surprisingly, Gerald Manning.

I have mentioned our 1962 preparations for the launching of Norfolk Opera Players. Launching somehow seems appropriate because our first performance was at Cromer Pier Pavilion, then owned by Tom Bolton.

In later years, I wrote some verses about Norfolk Opera Players. It might save me a few paragraphs if I quoted two of the verses now:-

FROM THE BEGINNING

In Norfolk, 'back in nineteen sixty-two
Music was being made; and art and sculpture
Were manifest, so that one knew
That there was more than agri-culture.
But though 'The Wells' would travel *Traviata*,
The Barber, La Bohème and things like this,
For Pergolesi's *Frate 'nnamorato*
You'd have to search the great Metropolis,
So that is why there entered now the lists,
Determined to fulfil this long felt want,
Those tilting, lilting, musical masochists
Presenting to the world their debutant(e)
Pooling a trifle of their hard-earned cash,
Needing of Mother Luck more than a drop of her,
They entered the arena with panache
And fittingly performed *The Beggar's Opera*-
Thus on this Gay delight they opened tabs,
To sing, cavort and generally roister,
First playing in the wake of Cromer crabs,
Then opening up the Maddermarket oyster.
Thieves, trollops, fence (and jailer for expedience}
Made merry in this wondrous Newgate ballad,
Setting the style, providing the ingredients
For future mixtures of the NOPera salad.

The Cromer performance went extremely well. It was produced by Geoffrey Clarke and conducted by Frederick Firth. George James had been involved in early music training and advice. Having used the words 'extremely well', I perhaps ought to add that this euphoric result was reached in spite of Audrey, as Mrs Peachum, sipping a little too much of Eric Hartley's home-made raspberry wine ('I was always very curious in my liquors' she utters) and missing out a couple of paragraphs of the libretto; also that the orchestra managed very well under the leadership of Hilary Gostling, despite the absence one evening of the second violin, Margaret Bidwell, who had gone out with the lifeboat. Deserving of mention, also, is my playing of the coconut shells depicting my arrival on horseback prior to stage entry, undoubtedly leaving the audience to wonder at my ability to ride on water.

'Opening up the Maddermarket Oyster' in the above verse perhaps needs a little clarification. Up to this time, the Maddermarket Theatre had been the exclusive domain of the Norwich Players, although the reader will recall that a joint enterprise between them and the Norfolk & Norwich Amateur Operatic Society had previously presented *The Beggar's Opera*. Well, in consultation with Ian Emmerson, artistic director of that establishment at a luncheon arranged by Eric Hartley, who was a member of both societies, we repeated the opera there in October, this time under the baton of George James. In one sequence of the opera, the Ladies of the Town, responding to the director's instructions, launched themselves amorously at me, resulting in my being completely submerged by eight 'ladies'. (Alas, I do not recall this happening to me in real life). Anyway, disengaging myself ultimately from the entanglement, I stood up and inadvertently said: 'Where was I?' The audience were kind enough to laugh. This venture (the opera, I mean) was to be the first of a series of small operas presented there in the ensuing years.

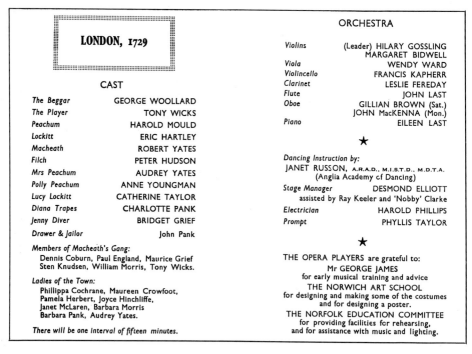

LONDON, 1729

CAST

The Beggar	GEORGE WOOLLARD
The Player	TONY WICKS
Peachum	HAROLD MOULD
Lockitt	ERIC HARTLEY
Macheath	ROBERT YATES
Filch	PETER HUDSON
Mrs Peachum	AUDREY YATES
Polly Peachum	ANNE YOUNGMAN
Lucy Lockitt	CATHERINE TAYLOR
Diana Trapes	CHARLOTTE PANK
Jenny Diver	BRIDGET GRIEF
Drawer & Jailor	John Pank

Members of Macheath's Gang:
Dennis Coburn, Paul England, Maurice Grief
Sten Knudsen, William Morris, Tony Wicks.

Ladies of the Town:
Phillippa Cochrane, Maureen Crowfoot,
Pamela Herbert, Joyce Hinchliffe,
Janet McLaren, Barbara Morris
Barbara Pank, Audrey Yates.

There will be one interval of fifteen minutes.

ORCHESTRA

Violins	(Leader) HILARY GOSSLING
	MARGARET BIDWELL
Viola	WENDY WARD
Violincello	FRANCIS KAPHERR
Clarinet	LESLIE FEREDAY
Flute	JOHN LAST
Oboe	GILLIAN BROWN (Sat.)
	JOHN MacKENNA (Mon.)
Piano	EILEEN LAST

★

Dancing Instruction by:
JANET RUSSON, A.R.A.D., M.I.S.T.D., M.D.T.A.
(Anglia Academy cf Dancing)
Stage Manager DESMOND ELLIOTT
assisted by Ray Keeler and 'Nobby' Clarke
Electrician HAROLD PHILLIPS
Prompt PHYLLIS TAYLOR

★

THE OPERA PLAYERS are grateful to:
Mr GEORGE JAMES
for early musical training and advice
THE NORWICH ART SCHOOL
for designing and making some of the costumes
and for designing a poster.
THE NORFOLK EDUCATION COMMITTEE
for providing facilities for rehearsing,
and for assistance with music and lighting.

I have a programme and a Press critique of a performance of Mendelssohn's oratorio *St Paul* with the Sheringham & Cromer Choral society. I cannot remember learning this work, and I certainly forget its content, perhaps because that is the only occasion on which I sang it.

Hiawatha's Wedding Feast and Departure at Lowestoft featured Jane Manning, Peter Bamber and myself as soloists. The augmented Millard Tolhurst

Orchestra were led, as always, by Jack Goddard, and conducted by Claude Richards.

A recital at Wymondham Abbey included Hilary Gostling, violin, Norman Crowhurst, organ, and ourselves. I don't recall who sponsored this recital, but it seems that it was a bit up-market, because the charge for the programme, on a plain sheet of paper, was 2/6d.

The soloists for a concert version of *The Mikado* by the Norwich Union Choral Society were, with the exception of Audrey singing the role of Katisha, all employees of Norwich Union. Joan Brooks was again the accompanist and George James the conductor.

The cast of *The Gondoliers* at Lowestoft included a young mezzo-soprano Bridget Bartlam, who became a professional singer. Apart from other familiar names, Frank Williamson (well-known in Cromer) sang the role of the Duke of Plazatoro.

Audrey sang in the performance of Bach's *Christmas Oratorio* with the King's Lynn Musical Society augmented by the Downham Musical Society. The other soloists were Derek Roper, tenor and William Lloyd, bass, neither of whom are known to me.

I later learned that Peter Bamber was, with Jane, a pupil of Eric Greene.

Macheath with the Ladies of the Town
By courtesy of Eastern Counties Newspapers

Chapter 17 - 1964

Muriel Smith Recital (St Andrew's Hall, Norwich) ~ Recital (Assembly House, Norwich) ~ Bach's *Sleepers Wake* and Haydn's *Third Mass* (Beccles Church) ~ *St John Passion* (St Alban's Church, Norwich) ~ *Merrie England* (concert version) (Stuart Hall, Norwich) ~ *Merrie England* (concert version) (Dereham Memorial Hall) ~ Handel's *Passion According to St John* (St Peter Mancroft Church, Norwich) ~ *Songs of the Fleet*, Haydn's *The Seasons* and *Liebeslieder Waltzes* (Farlingaye School Hall, Woodbridge) ~ *Creation* (Thorpe St Andrew's Church) ~ Concert (Thetford Guildhall) ~ Brahms' *Requiem* (Grammar School Hall, Great Yarmouth) ~ Concert (Town hall, Great Yarmouth) ~ *Patience* (Cromer Pier Pavilion) ~ *Messiah* (Cromer Parish Church) ~ Recital (Sampford Brett) ~ Opera Highlights (Stuart Hall, Norwich) ~ Elizabethan Evening (Norwich Castle Keep) ~ *Merry Wives of Windsor* (The Maddermarket Theatre) Norwich ~ *Acis and Galatea* (King's Lynn Technical College) ~ Christmas Concert (St Andrew's Hall, Norwich)

It might have been around this time that Lady Somerleyton 'phoned and asked me to sing at a Sunday service in Somerleyton Church. Audrey had already met Lady Somerleyton through her work as Craft Organiser for the Disabled, having sales of work at her garden openings. I presented myself in good time, negotiating a driveway about a mile long. I pulled the front door bell, but getting no response, opened the door and found myself in a vast hall full of gigantic stuffed bears. Lord and Lady Somerleyton, his sister from Harringfleet Hall nearby, the Somerleyton's younger son and his fiancée were discovered behind one of the bears, having afternoon tea (to which I had been invited). It looked a sort of Teddy Bear's Picnic, although the bears were not eating. It was all pretty overpowering, but I ate my bread and strawberry jam with as much aplomb as I could muster, and off we went to church. I sang two solos, Handel's 'Largo' and one of Sarastro's arias from the *Magic Flute*, with the words 'Thou Art, O God' (I never had much of a repertoire of religious songs outside oratorio arias). It went well. I had been invited to dinner as well, and the other guest was the Reverend Bill Westwood (later Bishop) whom Audrey and I had known through our performances at St Margaret's Church, Lowestoft. We drank sherry in the library and Lord Somerleyton stood at the doorway to collect our glasses as we proceeded to the dining room. I was placed next to his sister. We ate Somerleyton pears with a knife and fork and Lady X asked me whether we had a garden and grew any fruit. 'Yes,' I replied, 'mainly Bramleys.' I don't think that this fulfilled Lady X's expectations of me. She had another try 'Are you related to the Hampshire Yates's?' Wisely, I didn't qualify my reply in the negative with 'probably Liverpool–Irish'. Another difficult moment was when a discussion ensued over the wartime generals, and I ventured to comment that Montgomery wasn't very popular with the troops. *I* wasn't very popular then - I deduced that Montgomery was a friend.

In 1964 George Richards, our dentist, persuaded me to join him and his wife Molly in a visit to Westminster Theatre, London, to hear a Welsh male-voice choir. Audrey and I were duly driven to London by George and we enjoyed the choir. At the end of the programme, people of various nationalities, professions and employment presented themselves on stage to declare their devotion to God. The concert had been arranged by Moral Re-armament, a religious group developed from the earlier Oxford Group and given to bible readings in each other's homes. After the show, we were taken to their headquarters in Charles Square, and sat down to a meal at a long table, with Audrey placed next to the head man (president or managing director?). I was seated opposite Muriel Smith, a beautiful coloured lady who played *Carmen Jones* in the first American stage production of that operatic concoction. During the evening I was asked if N.O.Ps. would promote a song recital by Muriel Smith at St Andrew's Hall. I said we would, but that as a society we could not align ourselves with any sacred or sectarian organisation. It was agreed that no mention should be made of Moral Re-armament (although they would sponsor it). Muriel arrived on the morning of the performance and we laid on a lunch at the Royal Hotel (with Norfolk Opera Players paying for their own). With Muriel on my arm in the pre-meal assembly I felt very elated. In the evening she presented a beautiful recital. I presented a bouquet. Between lunch and performance Audrey and I hosted John Constable, her accompanist, even then of national repute. He elected to sleep and used our bed until teatime.

The programme for the following Recital does not indicate where it was performed. Could this have been the Assembly House? I have assumed so. Anyway, the performers were Dorothy Hughes, flute, Eileen Last, piano, Audrey and myself and Geoffrey Laycock, who I think accompanied us whilst Eileen accompanied Dorothy. My contribution included 'Largo al Factotum' once again.

The programme of Bach's *Sleeper's Wake*, and Haydn's *Third Mass* shows the same set of performers as for the previous Beccles concert. I recall that when Roland Reynolds rang to ask us to perform in any Mass, his Norfolk accent would come through – 'We're duin it in La'in'.

This would be the second occasion on which Audrey sang in a *St John Passion*, - this time with Walter Shackleton, tenor, George James, bass, (Jesus), Ina Roe, soprano, and Tony Faulkner, bass.

We sang in a concert version of *Merrie England* at Dereham Memorial Hall. Barbara Fielden took the part of Bessie Throgmorton, with Audrey as Queen Elizabeth, I as Essex. In the finale of the first act Essex hands Bessie a letter. Concert versions are always compromises, so far as action is concerned, but on this occasion I decided to hand Bessie a simulated letter. I selected a coloured photograph of the interior of a stomach; Barbara didn't move a muscle – I giggled. Audrey and I took a one day trip to Venice in 1991, and at Venice Airport, a lady came up to me and said, 'You don't remember me, do you? The last time we met you handed me a coloured photograph of the interior of a stomach'.

On Palm Sunday, I sang in *The Passion According to St John* by Handel, in St Peter Mancroft Church, Norwich. Other soloists included Douglas Clarke, baritone, David Westgate, tenor and Ronald Goose, alto.

The Spring concert at Woodbridge conducted by Gordon Hawkins was composed of a strange mixture of items: 'Spring' from Haydn's *The Seasons*, Stanford's *Songs of the Fleet*, Brahms' *Liebeslieder Waltzes*, and excerpts from *The Beggar's Opera*.

The performance of Haydn's *Creation* at Thorpe Church brought back memories for me of my earlier years there as boy soloist and later (still pre-war) as bass soloist. This performance was a Norfolk Education Committee presentation, a sort of echo, I suppose of the *St Mathew Passion* occasions when many choirs were united in performance, for in this instance it was a combination of Thorpe St Andrew Church Choir, Thorpe Village W.I. Choir, Blofield Choral Society and North Walsham Choral Society, and the conductor was Douglas Coombes, then Sidney Twemlow's deputy. Other soloists were Alice Peters, soprano and Anthony Severn, tenor. Reginald Bolton was the organist.

A concert to which we contributed at Thetford Guildhall included Hector Sutherland whose band played at the Samson and Hercules ballroom before the war.

Norfolk Opera Players was becoming a large company, since the nature of what we were performing attracted singers. We needed therefore to move from ballad opera to larger works, and it seemed that this should be accomplished first by performing a Gilbert & Sullivan opera. We chose *Patience* and I negotiated with the Town Council to present once more at the Pier Pavilion. The Town Council had now purchased the concert hall from Tom Bolton. The performance was a success and, as usual on these occasions we repaired to the nearby pub to celebrate – mildly of course, though the drink and drive restrictions were not yet being enforced. Other local patrons of the establishment not having to travel, did not need to observe a strict discipline, made manifest by one gentleman, who approached us one evening along the long entrance corridor, fell flat on his face, turned his face upwards and beamed, and said rather wetly, 'Good evening, all'.

> After the merry start, how best continue?
> *The Beggar* had enriched us in a sense;
> Experience gained, and at the second venue
> We profited in pounds instead of pence.
> Patience was needed, therefore *Patience* shown
> (And all our other sterling qualities too),
> Husbanding what we had already grown
> And sowing another fertile seed or two.
> Developmental rather than epochal
> It gave artistic outlet (or catharsis)

But several of the throats were streptococcal
And the dancing trio strained their metatarsus.

Brahms' *Requiem* and Bach's cantata *God so Loved the World* were performed at the Grammar School Hall, Great Yarmouth, and not the Town Hall, the Society's usual venue. Rita Green was the other soloist and the conductor Cyril Huggins.

I was at the Town Hall again in July however, contributing to a concert with two groups of songs and the baritone role in Stanford Robinson's *Plantation Songs* once more. Cyril Huggins accompanied my songs.

Another *Messiah* at Cromer was this time with Sheringham & Cromer Choral Society, Fakenham Choral Society, and St Mary's Choir, Norwich. Other soloists were Alice Thornton, soprano (wife of Harry Thornton, violin, previously referred to) and Richard White, tenor.

In the summer we went to Somerset again to stay with Charles and Evelyn in their vast rectory at Sampford Brett. These were long journeys avoiding motorways (if there were any then), but travel was infinitely more enjoyable. On one occasion at least we camped for the night on a wide grass verge in a side road, the girls occupying the car and Audrey and I sleeping in a tent borrowed from her brother. Imagine doing this nowadays. A Press cutting in my 1964 file reveals that Audrey and I sang in a recital of music in the church, together with other artistes, including Charles playing violin.

We joined the St Cecilia Chorus and Orchestra once again, in the company of Charlotte Pank and Anthony Severn, to sing excerpts from Grand Opera and from Gilbert and Sullivan operas.

Then, with Stanley Littlechild as tenor this time (I think), we sang under the name of 'The Anglia Madrigal Ensemble' (difficult now to believe) directed by Douglas Coombes. The occasion was an Elizabethan evening in the Norwich Castle Keep organised jointly by The Norfolk Education Drama Committee and The Maddermarket Theatre Association. We sang on the staircase.

Norfolk Opera Players were again at the Maddermarket presenting Nicolai's opera *The Merry Wives of Windsor* with a small orchestra. Daisy Brooks, nationally known for her miniature paintings, and sister of Joan Brooks who had accompanied us at the piano on several occasions, asked if she might tint a black and white photograph of Audrey and me in our stage costumes. The result is displayed in our music room at home. How I wish that I had grown my own beard, as I would do on several future occasions.

> We tilted next at a somewhat bolder target
> (*The Merry Wives* could well be labelled thus)
> Justice was done unto the Maddermarket,
> Will Shakespeare, Otto Nicolai and us.

Rita Green, Bernard Wesby and I were the soloists in a performance of Handel's *Acis and Galatea* at King's Lynn. The conductor of the combined choirs of King's Lynn Musical Society and Downham Society was once again Aubrey Hood.

Audrey sang in the St Andrew's Hall Christmas concert, which featured Part I of Bach's *Christmas Oratorio* and Part I of Handel's *Messiah*, concluding another busy year.

It was in this year that I went to hospital for a nose operation to remove polypi, which had troubled me for some time, and had been snared at Outpatients Surgery from time to time. The method was to apply a local anaesthetic to the back of the nose, by means of cotton wool stuffed into the nose with a steel rod about the length of a meat skewer, which had to be kept in place for a quarter of an hour. Then the specialist would cut the polyps with an instrument consisting of a snare on the end of a rod. On one such visit the anaesthetic had been applied, and I sat in the waiting room with the anaesthetic held in place by the steel rod, when a lady came in, looked at me and fainted. I've done nothing to cause ladies to faint (at least not from fright) since that occasion. Happily the hospital operation under general anaesthetic got rid of this problem.

The following is a verse penned (I forget by whom) in celebration of the success.

> Salutation, salutation
> To your nasal operation-
> To your bones re-cast.
> Approbation, approbation
> Of your new-found inhalation,
> Bone and polypi –
> Crop to multiply,
> Epic snores and quiv'ring doors –
> All is gone at last,
> Obstruction passed.
> We from Norfolk's Academe
> To realise the singer's dream
> Of joyous dawns and tuneful nights
> Do wish you new inspiring heights
> In the name of Academe.

Chapter 18 - 1965

The Banner of St. George and *Creation* (St Andrew's Hall, Norwich) ~
Carmen (concert version) (St Andrew's Hall, Norwich) ~ *Susannah's
Secret* (Maddermarket Theatre, Norwich) ~ *The Marriage* and *Tom
Jones* (Lowestoft C.W.S. Hall) ~ Maddermarket Music Hall

Eight Guild choirs took part in a Townswomens' Guild concert at St Andrew's
Hall, with soloists Ann Youngman, Anthony Wick and myself. The redoubtable
John Hammond was the pianist, and Colin Clouting led a string quartet, with
Mary Firth conducting. Ann Youngman and I contributed to Elgar's *The Banner
of St George* and the three of us performed in an abridged version of Haydn's
Creation; I don't think that anyone fainted on this occasion.

    I was privileged to join three professional soloists in a concert performance at
St Andrew's Hall of Bizet's *Carmen,* presented by the St Cecilia Chorus and
Orchestra, conducted by Hugh Skeens and led by Sylvia Shackleton. Jean
Allister sang the role of Carmen, Angela Jenkins that of Michaela, Thomas
Round was Don José and I was Escamillo.

By courtesy of Eastern Counties Newspapers

**Left to Right: Robert Yates, Angela Jenkins,
Jean Allister, Thomas Round**

73

This was a year of much fewer engagements than usual, but we (the Norfolk Opera Players) presented *Susannah's Secret* (Wolfe Ferarri) and *The Marriage* (Martinu) at the Maddermarket Theatre. These two performances are amongst my happiest memories of the NOP performances.

From a Press critique it appears that we were again at Lowestoft, performing a concert version of Edward German's *Tom Jones* although I can't find a programme. Interesting to note however that Bob Richardson, that well-known Hethersett bass, was singing Squire Weston, as I recall, at my instigation.

Also in this year we were lured into performing in the Maddermarket Music Hall, with performances on Boxing Day, New Year's Eve, and a week's performance in the New Year. Audrey and I were called 'The Aspidistras' and for the next twenty years we were to be associated with this event. We lampooned Victorian duets, dressed appropriately, and in the early days, had a great deal of fun. We were always the penultimate act and always well received. Our party pieces included such songs (arranged as duets) as Tosti's 'Parted' in which we would get dreadfully tangled up, Tosti's 'Goodbye', where we were pinned together to make separation impossible, 'Farewell in the Desert' with Audrey in scant attire as a lady of the harem and I as a lascivious sheikh, and several other duets fraught with various problems.

By courtesy of Eastern Counties Newspapers

Eight choirs of the Townswomen's Guild conducted by Mary Firth

Chapter 19 - 1966

The Redeemer (Tacket Street Congregational Church, Ipswich) ~
King Arthur (concert version) (Gresham's School, Holt) ~
Engaged (Thorpe Grammar School) *Messiah* (St Nicholas Church,
Great Yarmouth) ~ *Messiah* (Dereham Memorial Hall) ~ Victorian
Evening (Norwich Castle) ~ Vivaldi's *Gloria* (St Nicholas Church, North
Walsham) *The Strife is O'er* and Spring from Haydn's *The Seasons*
(Tacket Street Congregational) ~ *Messiah* (Corn Exchange, Ipswich) ~
Christmas Music, inc. *The Nativity* (Town Hall, Great Yarmouth) ~
Elephant in Arcady (Maddermarket Theatre, Norwich) ~
Maddermarket Music Hall.

On 6th March, Gordon Hawkins enticed us to Ipswich once more, this time to participate in Martin Shaw's *The Redeemer*, classified as a Lenten Oratorio. I have mentioned Martin Shaw earlier and our meeting with him at the Assembly House. His name is also significant to me, in that I sang one of his songs in a Birmingham broadcast, a setting of Shakespeare's words 'Full Fathom Five'. It is also significant to observe in the programme of *The Redeemer* that his life span was 1875–1958, so that he lived only two years after we met him in Norwich.

I remember that *King Arthur* (March 13th) at Gresham's, included a frost scene in which the Cold Genius (me) was required to sing with a 'shake', I had to practice this.

From March 16th to 19th we (NOPs) presented *Engaged* at Thorpe Grammar School. This Gilbert and Sullivan concoction needed a larger stage than the Maddermarket. In opera and operetta the low-voiced ladies are usually cast in older or rather unattractive roles. *Engaged* was an exception, which enabled Audrey to be cast as the leading lady, Belinda. Geoffrey Clarke produced, and Frederick Firth was musical director.

Messiah ('slightly abridged', the March 24th programme says) at Great Yarmouth was interesting in that the soprano solos were taken by a boy treble, the reason no doubt being that this was a performance by Duncan Hall and Taverham Hall School choirs. Looking at the items listed I note that No.6. ('But who may abide') and No.40 ('Why do the nations') are both missing. I think it is reasonable to suppose that the organ accompanist (Gerald Matthews) was aware of the problems presented in the accompaniments of these two items.

The *Messiah* at Dereham (April 1st) obviously presented no such problems for David Kett, organist on that occasion, because both Nos.6 and 40 were included. Fred Andrews provided the trumpet work in 'The Trumpet Shall Sound' and the programme shows 'Timpani – John McKenna'.

The Victorian Evening surely must have been inspired by the success of the earlier Elizabethan Evening, both held at Norwich Castle. It was presented by the Chairman, Marguerite Lady Hastings, on behalf of the Norfolk Drama Committee and the Maddermarket Theatre Association, on 29th April. All sorts of groups appear to have contributed to dance, drama and musical presentations

By courtesy of Eastern Counties Newspapers

Audrey as Belinda in *Engaged* with (left to right) Anthony Wick, Robert Yates and John Dunsire

Our contribution (Mesdames Rita Green and Audrey Yates and Messrs Robert Yates and Anthony Wick with accompanists Mesdames Eileen Last and Ann Coombes) seems to have been made under the title of 'The Windsor Quartet' (singers). The music of the evening was arranged by Douglas Coombes. The quartets listed in the programme are unknown to me now, but we must have sung them. I do remember, however that our audience didn't think much of it, because most of them moved across to dramatic presentations which were being performed at the same time, and obviously had a more compelling charm.

The North Walsham concert contained pieces for choir, orchestra, congregation and organ, and in its second half Vivaldi's *Gloria*. The name of the orchestra is not given, nor the names of its members. Douglas Coombes conducted and Kenneth Condon was the organist. The singers in the *Gloria* were Rita Green, Valerie Drury and Audrey Yates.

The Strife is O'er is a cantata for Soprano, Tenor and Bass soloists, chorus and organ, and, as I pen this, it is interesting to note that it is by Raymond Warren, ex-professor of Bristol University Music Department, whom I was destined to meet when performing in one of his major works in a later year. This 1966 occasion included also a performance of the 'Spring' section of Haydn's *The Seasons*.

The *Messiah* in Ipswich Corn Hall was with the Ipswich Choral Society and the Ipswich Orchestral Society, conductor Paul Hardeman. Richard White was the tenor, and the lady soloists were unknown to me and were either professionals or local singers. The word 'professional' is used by me rather reluctantly and is not intended to convey the feeling that a local 'amateur' was in a kind of second division. Not so; it is merely that they earn their living (or try to) by singing. There are good and ordinary professionals and good and ordinary amateurs and comparisons might sometimes be in favour of the latter.

The Nativity by Elizabeth Poston is described as 'A Sequence for Christmas'. The Yarmouth performance included Rita Green as the soprano soloist and Audrey as the contralto. Both also sang songs.

In order to keep Opera Players busy, I arranged for *Elephant in Arcady* (music by Mozart, adapted by Ernest Irving) to be performed at the Maddermarket Theatre. I remember this chiefly for the mini-smocks we wore as Arcadian Shepherds. Not a pretty sight.

The Aspidistras, of whom I have already given some account, was one of many acts included in the end-of-year performances at the Maddermarket. Regular contributors were Rita Green and Peter Hudson, with whom Audrey and I were 'entangled' in various quartets, rendered both vocally and physically. Others were George Baker, Sylvia Dix, Adrian Wright, Bridget Grief, Roger Lloyd, Albert Cooper and Norma Wick. Jonathon Meddings and Ian Emmerson (the producers) also contributed. Many others were involved, and new faces would appear each year. At the risk of offending those who appeared only rarely on these occasions (some of whose names I forget) I will refrain from mentioning the few names I remember.

I must, however, give special mention to Norma Wick. She was always last on the bill of fame, and rightly so. In earlier days of course Norma had been leading lady in many Norfolk and Norwich Amateur Operatic Society performances, but she brought an outstanding talent to music hall songs. Norma had such magic that she would appear, scan the audience superciliously, and have them in stitches without uttering a word, and when a word came, it would not 'normally' be flattering.

All of these performances, as mentioned, were accompanied by the indefatigable Eileen Last, tireless in her exacting task of meeting the requirements of the performers' interpretations.

Chapter 20 - 1967

Maddermarket Music Hall ~ Bach's *B Minor Mass* (St Edmund's Catholic Church, Bury St.Edmunds) ~ *Messiah* (Central Hall, Deneside, Great Yarmouth) ~ *Merrie England* (concert version) (Co-operative Hall, Lowestoft) ~ Spring Concert (inc. *Plantation Songs*) (Dereham Boy's Secondary Modern School) ~ *A Time for Growing* (St Andrew's Hall, Norwich for theTriennial Festival) ~ Handel's *Sixth Chandos Anthem* (Cromer Church) ~ Mozart's *First Mass In C* ~ Recital (Sir John Leman School, Beccles) ~ *La Perichole* (Theatre Royal, Norwich) ~ Concert (Townswomen's Guild) (St Andrew's Hall, Norwich) ~ Recital (St Edmunds Church, Acle) Christmas Music (St Margaret's Church, Lowestoft) ~ Bach's *Cantata No.158* (University of East Anglia) ~ Christmas Music inc. *The New Born King*, (Town Hall, Great Yarmouth) ~ Maddermarket Music Hall.

I believe that it was the popularity of the recent annual performance of Old Time Music Hall at the Maddermarket that inspired Ian Emmerson to expand this offering to 'Melodrama and Music Hall', presented this year from January 13th to January 21st, with two matinées. The drama element was represented by *Ten Nights in a Bar Room* by William W. Pratt, directed by Ian Emmerson, with décor by Anna Welbourne. Anna was the superb artist (and a lovely lady) who served the Maddermarket Theatre for so many years in this capacity. The programme shows that Audrey and I (as The Aspidistras) sang Tosti's 'Parted'. This was a send-up as before, which tied us in awful tangles, and was to be repeated many times over the ensuing years. A word about the 'Maddermarket Glee Singers', also listed. Anonymity was the Maddermarket rule in those days, but I can reveal that these performers were Mesdames Rita Green and Audrey Yates, and Messrs Peter Hudson and Robert Yates, and at the piano was Mistress Eileen Last (listed as Mistress Eileen Earl). Our contributions over the years included a quartet called 'Gathering up Shells from the Shore' and a rendition of a setting by M. W. Balfe of Longfellow's 'Excelsior'. Jonathan Meddings staged all of these items, and spared us nothing in the very physical interpretation of them.

Richard White asked me to sing with him in a performance of Bach's *B Minor Mass* at St Edmund's Catholic Church, Bury St. Edmunds. The other three soloists were professionals. We sang from the gallery at the West End with a small choir and an orchestral ensemble. Apparently this was the first time for countless years that any Mass had been presented liturgically in the church. This was also the first time I had been present at a Roman Catholic Church service. There was much incense, with priests genuflecting in tandem.

Bernard Wesby and I joined two ladies not known to me, before or since, in another performance of the *Messiah* with the Duncan Hall and Taverham Hall School Choirs, this time augmented by members of the Great Yarmouth Musical

Society. Once again, 'But who may abide' and 'Why do the Nations' were omitted.

A concert version of *Merrie England* at Lowestoft was one of those very rare occasions when I had to withdraw because of a throat infection. A replacement was found by Jane Manning (now a professional singer) who was singing the soprano role. He was a professional singer (and ex-professional footballer) called (Jeffery) Neilson Taylor, known as 'Jeff' Taylor when he played for Fulham (1st Division), and is now a respected voice teacher. He sang the part of Essex extremely well.

Audrey and I contributed two groups of songs each in a spring concert at Dereham. Douglas Coombes had now become the musical director of the Mid-Norfolk Choral Society following the departure of Edwin Kennedy. Our contributions were accompanied by Eileen Last, and once again I provided the solo baritone work in Stanford Robinson's *Plantation Songs*, which was accompanied by Mrs. D.C.P. Woolls.

The Triennial Festival of this year included a large-scale work by Anthony Hopkins, involving school choirs, nine soloists and an eighty-piece students' orchestra. One of the soloists was Angela Beale (soprano) with whom I had sung earlier in the year, in the Bach *B Minor Mass* at Bury St Edmunds; she became a well-known mezzo. The event took place in St Andrew's Hall, with atmospheric scenes projected on to a large screen behind the performers. The work was conducted by its composer, and produced by Ian Emmerson. I enjoyed working with Anthony Hopkins, and this occasion would be the first of several musical occasions on which we would meet. My part in this unusual drama was that of Lucretius, Roman poet and Epicurean philosopher. I had some nice pieces to sing, and the event was memorable. *Time for Growing* was a massive undertaking involving children from twenty-one schools, and a speaking chorus of pupils and staff from two more. In addition to the young orchestra were pianist Eileen Last (née Bidwell) and organist Cyril Pearce. Audience capacity was accordingly reduced by at least half. The work was directed towards showing that throughout man's time on earth there has been unresolved conflict between his desire for knowledge and truth on the one hand, and his eternal search for faith in a divine being on the other.

Audrey sang in a Choral and Organ Recital at Cromer Church, which included Handel's *Sixth Chandos Anthem*. This contralto aria would originally have been sung by a male alto, but even for such a voice, the singing line must be one of the lowest Handel ever wrote, and I think that there were not many other contraltos around who could have sung it.

We were at Beccles again in a song recital for the Beccles and District Arts Society accompanied by Eileen Last. We each sang twelve songs. I have mentioned the society's secretary Roland Reynolds before. Following the afternoon rehearsal, whether in St Edmunds or other churches or at Sir John Leman School, as it was on this occasion, Roland would stay behind to arrange things for the evening performance. Audrey and I (sometimes accompanied by our two daughters) would, upon his wife Winifred's invitation, repair to their abode to partake of tea, and also to change into evening clothes for the evening performance. On one such occasion, (it might have been this), Roland was a little late coming home, so Win decided to start tea without him. She produced some Christmas cake and, when I expressed surprise that cake could last this long (it was now October) she said that it wasn't a last Christmas cake, but the year before, and, since it contained brandy and had been stored in an airtight tin, it would be as good as new. She was wrong! Fortunately she had disappeared into the kitchen, enabling me to remove the offending concoction (I can re-live that taste today) and stuff it into my dress pocket-handkerchief. Upon her return, I simulated chewing movements, and expressed suitable polite epithets of appreciation. I had to ensure that I never touched that handkerchief during the evening's performance. I did not, but managed to do so upon arrival home, when I trod it into the lounge carpet.

Another interesting feature of the Reynolds' household was that the toilet was lit by a torch bulb. Let not these reminiscences cloud the fact that Roland and Win were a very nice couple, and we owed much to their generous hospitality.

Norfolk Opera Players were still increasing its membership. Never before had a local society produced operatic works more demanding than Gilbert and Sullivan's masterpieces, so ambitious local singers were avidly joining our ranks. The general feeling was that we should now venture forth with a production at the Theatre Royal. Modestly we chose Offenbach's *La Perichole*. For this production we were joined by Norwich Ballet Club. Their indomitable director and motivator, Margot Warne, joined me in persuading four members of the Norwich Priory Gymnasium to contribute to the production. I was also able to recruit the Norfolk Army Cadet Force, so that with gymnasts tumbling all over the place, the Cadet Force marching, and the Ballet club balleting, we presented a kind of musical extravaganza. It was a great success.

> With intrepidity we took a ballot
> To choose the Theatre as our venue,
> And there to titillate the palate
> We put *La Perichole* upon the menu.
> Music by Offenbach the only ploy
> To bring our venture to the public ear
> (But there was also ballet to enjoy
> And Priory Gym gymnasts extraordinaire).

Twelve Guild choirs contributed to a concert at St Andrew's Hall presented by the East Anglia Federation of Townswomen's Guilds. As ever it was conducted by Mary Firth, with John Hammond at the piano. Sally Stock and I were soloists.

A recital Audrey and I gave at Acle church enabled me to re-establish contact with the organist Arthur Daniels with whom I had sung so often at Thorpe church in pre-war days, both as boy and man.

The Lowestoft concert included Part I of the *Messiah*, and Vaughan Williams' *Fantasia on Christmas Carols* to which I contributed the baritone solos.

LA PÉRICHOLE
Cast in order of appearance

Estrella	VERA BUCKELL
Guadalena (The Three Cousins)	BRIDGET ROPER
Virginella	AUDREY YATES
Don Pedro de Hinoyosa (Governor of Lima)	JEREMY ANDREWS
The Count of Panatellas (First Gentleman of the Bedchamber)	PETER HUDSON
Don Andres de Ribeira (Viceroy of Peru)	ROBERT YATES
Paquillo	ANTONY SEVERN
La Perichole	ANN YOUNGMAN
First Notary	STEN KNUDSEN
Second Notary	DENNIS COWBURN
Ninetta	MARGUERITE COLE
Brambilla (The Ladies in Waiting)	INA BULLEN
Frasquinella	CATHERINE TAYLOR
Manuelita	SALLY STOCK
The Marquis de Tarapote (Lord Chancellor)	ERIC HARTLEY
The Old Prisoner	MAURICE GRIEF
The Turnkey	PERCY ASH

CHORUS OF COURTIERS, DRAGOONS, GRENADIERS AND PEOPLE

LADIES: Pamela Cowburn, Yvonne Ireson, Janet King, Pat Leggett, Muriel Margetson, Jean Meek, Barbara Morris, Janet Shreeve, Barbara Smith, Mildred Topliss-Green, Gwenneth Walker, Sian Wilson-Price.

GENTLEMEN: Percy Ash, Barry Brown, Dennis Cowburn, Kenneth Davis, Paul England, Eric Hartley, Maurice Grief, Sten Knudsen, William Morris, Richard Mitchell, Anthony Williams.

MARCHING SOLDIERS

Are all members of the Norfolk Army Cadet Force and appear by kind permission of the County Commandant Lt.-Colonel F. C. Atkinson.

"LADIES OF THE COURT BALLET"

Janice Baker, Sarah Baker, Norma Baxter, Jean Carter, Hazel Magnus, Sheila Mosley, Jane Macdonald, Linda Palmer, Eileen Pennington, Dawn Peters, Margaret Taylor, Angela Willis (Bear).

ACROBATS

Colin Askham, Bernard Robinson, John Lemon, Richard Prior, Simon Jenkinson (Clown)

ORCHESTRA

First Violins	Hilary Gossling (leader), Frederick Firth, Sylvia Jones, Vivienne McCubbin
	Jean Pope, Margaret Dye, Joyce Rickells, Jean Sargent
Second Violins	Sylvia Ord, Wendy Ward, John Lobel
Violas	Francis Kappher, Herbert Hood
'Cellos	Colin Goodchild
Bass	John Last, Dorothy Hughes
Flutes	Paul Andrews, John Rose
Oboes	David Watering, Christopher Chandler
Clarinets	June Emerson
Bassoon	Geoffrey Emerson, Jeremy Day, Peter Wheales, Stephen Cullington
Horns	Kingsley Norton, John Neal
Trumpets	Derek Aldred, Anthony Ronaldson, Alwyn Green
Trombones	Jacqueline Kendle
Percussion	
Conducted by	Douglas Coombes

Scenery built and painted by the company under the direction of Robin and Julia Newson. Ladies' costumes (players) and acrobats' costumes designed by Jonathan Meddings and made by ladies of the Norfolk Opera Players. Ladies' costumes (dancers) designed by Margot Warne and made by members of the Norwich Ballet Club. Men's costumes (players and marching soldiers) by S. B. Watts Ltd., Manchester. Additional lighting by Norfolk Drama Committee. Rehearsal arrangements under the Norfolk Education Committee's evening institute facilities. Poster design by Ted Fleetwood. Furniture in public square by Mr. and Mrs. A. W. Anderson, The Gatehouse Public House, Norwich. Flowers by Pettits of Reedham Ltd.

FOR NORFOLK OPERA PLAYERS

General Manager	ROBERT YATES
Stage Manager	ROBIN NEWSON
Assistant Stage Managers	PETER GRIFFITHS, DAVID GRUNDY, JOHN ROPER
Wardrobe Mistress	PAMELA COWBURN
Assistant Wardrobe Mistress	HELEN GRIFFITHS
Make-up	MAUREEN CROWFOOT
Hair Styling	BABARA MORRIS
Rehearsal Accompanists	EILEEN LAST, PATRICK KING
Prompt	JANE KNUDSEN

FULLY LICENSED BARS IN STALLS AND GRAND CIRCLE

81

Anthony Wick, tenor, and Andrée Maillard Back, soprano, Audrey and I were the *Messiah* soloists.

I was asked to sing the bass solo in Bach's *Cantata No.158*, 'Die Freide sei mit mur', at a concert presented by the U.E.A. Student's Musical Society and the Norwich Citadel Band. The bass solo is a delight, and I shall always remember the superb playing of the violin obligato by a charming student Mary Wray. I don't know whether she aspired to a musical career, but whether as amateur or professional, I am sure she must have been very successful.

I was engaged to sing the baritone solos in Gordon Jacob's work entitled *The New Born King*. The conductor was Cyril Huggins, and the two pianists performing the piano duets included in the work were Harold Starling and Patricia Ayton. Harold Starling, excellent as ever, accompanied me in a group of songs.

Maddermarket Music Hall completed the year's musical commitments.

NORFOLK & NORWICH
TRIENNIAL FESTIVAL OF MUSIC & THE ARTS 1967

'A TIME
FOR GROWING'

by Antony Hopkins
Libretto by Nesta Pain
Produced by Ian Emmerson

ST. ANDREW'S HALL

Monday, Tuesday & Wednesday
5th, 6th, 7th June
at 7.30 p.m.

Chapter 21 - 1968

Handel's *Chandos Anthem No. 6* and Haydn's *Theresa Mass* (Beccles) ~ *Pirates of Penzance* (concert version) (Sparrow's Nest Theatre, Lowestoft) ~ Concert (Stuart Hall, Norwich) ~ Music for Fun (Public Library, Great Yarmouth) ~ *Orpheus in the Underworld* (Theatre Royal, Norwich) ~ Grand Charity Concert (Theatre Royal, Norwich) ~ Maddermarket Music Hall.

This seems to have been a fairly light year, with only six concerts to record.

At Beccles we sang in Handel's *Chandos Anthem No.6*, with Audrey again plumbing the vocal depths in her solo. Also in the programme was Haydn's. *Theresa Mass*. Other soloists were Beryl Mann and Walter Shackleton.

The concert version of *Pirates of Penzance* was at Sparrow's Nest, a change from South Pier Pavilion and other Lowestoft venues. The cast, with one exception, had all been introduced to the society by me. The one exception was Martyn Hill, (see *Merrie England* previous chapter) singing Frederick, who had been introduced by Jane Manning, who was singing Mabel. Others were Sally Stock, Bob Richardson, Ken Davis and Anthony Wick, and our humble selves. Claude Richards was conducting and Michael Cole, then Anglia Television presenter, was Narrator.

The Stuart Hall concert with the Norwich Singers must have been the occasion of my first meeting with Dennis Johnson, who was conducting. We were to join forces on future occasions. I sang two groups of songs, and the baritone solos in Stanford Robinson's *Plantation Songs* once again.

'Music for Fun' in the Lecture Hall of the Public Library at Great Yarmouth was presented by the Great Yarmouth Musical Society Male Singers. The programme shows 'The Gentlemen Singers' singing male-voice arrangements of well-known songs, the 'Anglia Recorder Consort', piano duets by Harold Starling and Cyril Huggins, and yours truly contributing songs.

Orpheus in the Underworld was our Norfolk Opera Players' second production at the Theatre Royal. We were joined by The Norwich Ballet Club, and members of the Hewitt School Choir. Although I believe it met with reasonable acclaim, I don't think that it was a good choice, since we were not progressing towards grand opera, which was our intention. The following verse reflects my opinion at the time.

> Though Offenbach undoubtedly impressed,
> Should we his repertoire have further plundered?
> To can-can, caper, jollify and jest
> Through *Orpheus in the Underworld?* – I wondered.

With Norfolk Opera Players, my self-imposed duties of 'running the show' became a way of life, together with my salaried occupation. Audrey had developed a craft scheme for the Norfolk Association for the Care of the

Handicapped, starting from a minuscule affair and developing it to a very substantial enterprise making constant demands on her time outside normal working hours. Our social hours were therefore interspersed with the many requirements of these two enterprises. Our daughters meanwhile were pursuing their musical studies with piano lessons from Joan Roe.

The Norfolk Association referred to above, involved the supply of material to handicapped people, teaching them a craft, and then selling their products, giving them physical and mental occupation, with a certain monetary reward and a pride of achievement. As with all voluntary associations, funds were limited, which prompted me, in this year, to organise a Grand Charity Concert at the Theatre Royal in November.

Norfolk Opera Players took part, together with Norwich Singers, Hewitt School Choir, Duncan Hall School Choir, Norwich Mozart Orchestra, Norwich Wind Band, and members of Norwich Players. Guest artiste was Antony Hopkins and the compère was John Bassett, then announcer for Anglia Television. With this formidable number of bodies to manage, I devised a schedule whereby one unit would succeed another on stage with military precision, so that there was space in the wings and the band-room below stage to facilitate the flow. I think the general order for each unit was band-room, wings (stage left), stage, exit stage right to band-room. Audrey had been busy, persuading Colin Chapman (of Lotus Cars) to donate a Mini-van for the use of N.A.D. staff. The van was pushed on to the stage during the concert and

The Aspidistras 1968

presented formally to the president of the Society, Lady Priscilla Bacon. The tickets were priced at £1, 12s., and 7s. and the Society profited by £500, a magnificent sum for that date.

Maddermarket Music Hall occupied us once again over the Christmas and New Year period. The photographs below show Audrey and myself as 'The Aspidistras' and as part of 'The Glee Singers' previously referred to. The feather in Audrey's hat menaced the ensemble from start to finish in one particular number. In a performance of 'Excelsior' we were roped together, wearing overcoats, scarves, boots, hats and gloves of the Victorian era in a scene simulating mountain climbing, with snow (actually washing powder) gently falling, and all of us getting into some frightful tangles, a fair representation, I think, of Longfellow's ridiculous poem.

Six school choirs participated in a carol concert at St Andrew's Hall on 1st December. It was organised by the British and Foreign Bible Societies (Norwich Auxiliary). Norwich Symphonic Wind were also featured as was Robert Norton, organist. Eileen Last was accompanist, and I sang solos. I am amazed to find that my contribution to this essentially sacred concert was:-

'Non Piu Andrai' – Mozart
'Song of the Flea' – Moussorgsky
'Sea Fever' – John Ireland
'The Old Superb' – Stanford.

The concert concluded with 'O Come all ye Faithful'!

I was asked to speak at a Cromer and Sheringham Operatic Society dinner, and mention this fact because Audrey and I had been such a part of music in this area.

The Christmas Concert presented by the Norwich City College Music Society included a performance of Bach's cantata *Sleepers Wake!* This must have been the reason for my inclusion. I think this must be the only occasion on which I have sung with Deirdre Cope, soprano. The bass and soprano duets in this work are very attractive. Ronald Watson was organist, (an important name in Norfolk music) and Howard Burrell (then teaching music at the college) conducted. The college choir and orchestra were led by Eric Burdett.

We took *Cox and Box* and excerpts from the *Pirates* to Norwich Prison to entertain the prisoners. A lady named Doreen Barber was at that time organising such events. Excerpts from the *Pirates* included the Policemen's chorus. No marks for guessing what ensued. Pandemonium. Additional warders were rushed in to guard doors and performers.

On an earlier occasion I had sung there with the Catton Choral Society in a performance of Haydn's *Creation*, would you believe it? One of the bass recitatives concludes, in a very low voice with the words 'in long dimensions creeps with sinuous trace, the worm'. It was then that I detected a chap in about the fifth row twigging the ear of the man in front. I think that it was more from a sense of humour than affront that I sustained the low note with my eyes fastened on him, until eventually he caught on and desisted.

Chapter 22 - 1969

Fauré's *Requiem* (St Peter Mancroft Church, Norwich) ~ Recital (Thorpe St Andrew Church, Norwich) ~ *Trial by Jury and H.M.S. Pinafore* (concert versions) (Sparrow's Nest Theatre, Lowestoft) ~ *The Deal and The Night Bell* (Maddermarket Theatre, Norwich) ~ Bach Cantata *God's Time is the Best* (Cromer Church) ~ *Creation* (St Mary the Virgin Church, Heacham) Recital (South Lowestoft Methodist Church) ~ Worstead Festival Recital (Worstead Church) ~ *Elijah* (St Mary's Baptist Church, Norwich) ~ *The Bartered Bride* (Theatre Royal, Norwich) ~ Carols and Music (St Andrew's Hall, Norwich) Cromer and Sheringham Operatic Dinner ~ Christmas Concert (inc. *Sleepers Wake*) (St Stephen's Church, Norwich.) ~ *Tyndale* (Cromer Church) ~ Grand Charity Concert (Theatre Royal) ~ Maddermarket Music Hall.

I sang in Fauré's *Requiem* at St Peter Mancroft Church with the Broadland Singers, with Mary Wells (professional soprano and wife of Philip Ledger, then in charge of music at the U.E.A.). The organist was Bernard Burrell, and Angela Dugdale conducted the choir. A small orchestra ensemble entitled The Mancroft Players contributed two Bach sonatas

Noel Watson, who had been my best man in 1947, invited me to sing in 'A Musical Celebration' in Thorpe Church, a thanksgiving for the Organ Restoration. Noel was then organist there.

We were at Sparrow's Nest Theatre, Lowestoft again with concert versions of *Trial By Jury* and *H.M.S. Pinafore.*

Keeping Norfolk Opera Players employed up to the maximum of their ability was my philosophy, and this meant two productions a year in order to use as much solo talent as possible. So we presented two more small operas at the Maddermarket Theatre. One was *The Night Bell* (Donizetti). Our friend Rita Green, with whom we had performed so much oratorio took the leading part in this one. Neither Audrey nor I was involved in this work, but we took leading parts in a small opera entitled *The Deal*, written for Norfolk Opera Players by Douglas Coombes. Douglas had been Assistant County Music Adviser in Norfolk before taking up a post as a B.B.C. Music Producer (Schools Radio), producing such well-known programmes as 'Singing Together'. Jane Manning tells me that she took part in some regular 'Singing Together' broadcasts for Douglas. The libretto of *The Deal* was based on a story by Guy de Maupassant. Others in the cast were Peter Hudson, Sally Stock, Mary Beverley, Nicholas Bloom, Roy Emerson, Stan Knudsen, Christopher Millett and Julia Yates (our younger daughter). (Mary Beverley became a professional singer for a while, performing Early Music. Peter Spalding (well respected for his drama productions at Keswick College) was producer, and the piano accompanist was the ubiquitous Eileen Last.

Maddermarket was not yet forsaken –
Pristine, but greatly atmospheric;
Perfect environment to reawaken
Our minds to thoughts of shows more esoteric.
So choosing *The Night Bell* by Donizetti
Together with *The Deal* by Douglas Coombes
We revelled in the music and libretti
Though takings scarcely heralded a boom.

The Broadland Singers, conducted by Angela Dugdale, presented a lyric drama concerning the life and death of William Tyndale (1494-1536). The narration was by Jonathon Meddings (of Maddermarket fame) and I sang the part of Tyndale. Happily, it was a concert version, so I escaped being strangled and burnt as a heretic. Brian Runnett was organist. Apart from his work as organist of Norwich Cathedral, he had a national reputation. Sadly, he was to die shortly afterwards in a car crash.

The Norfolk Singers with the County Staff String Quartet presented a programme at Cromer Church with Audrey and myself as soloists. I can't recall the Norfolk Singers being featured in any other performance, so I think this must have been an ad hoc venture directed by Emyr Evans, who had now become Assistant County Music Adviser. The instrumentalists were a splendid unit consisting of Paul Clarke, Margaret Crofts (violinists), Harry Thornton (playing viola on this occasion) and Barry Wright ('cello). The items performed were compositions of the 16th and 19th centuries. Our contribution was in Bach's Cantata *God's Time is the Best.*

We performed all three parts of Haydn's *Creation* at Heacham. It was more usual to omit Part III, because of the length of the complete work. However, so far as I can remember, the audience survived it. Perhaps they brought cushions. The performance was sung to organ accompaniment, the organist being Aubrey Hood, with whom we had been associated in King's Lynn performances, Aubrey was organist at Bury St Edmunds Cathedral. The conductor was Wilfred Copestake who himself was a splendid bass singer.

The Adam and Eve duet in Part III of the *Creation* contains the words, often repeated, 'Ev'ry moment spells new rapture'. I have a Novello edition of the vocal score where one of the repeats prints 'rupture' instead of 'rapture'. The previous owner of this volume has inserted a note 'Beware Adam'!

Our daughter Elizabeth was at this time attending Music College at Colchester and studying piano and voice. Earlier on, whilst at Wymondham College, she had been learning oboe, but this I think was now discarded, a fact which at least relieved us of the expense of continually sending for oboe reeds, which were posted to us in a small tobacco tin.

Julia also attended Wymondham College and later on the Blyth School (now the Blyth-Jex), she being taught flute by David Watering (previously referred to). Later still she attended Norwich City College.

We arranged a recital at South Lowestoft Methodist Church, which involved Liz and Julia. Liz did a reading (I think she did not yet feel confident enough to play piano or sing) and Julia played a flute sonatina. Anthony Wick and Rita Green were also present. Anthony Wick had been performing with us in N.O.P. productions and was a talented performer. Eileen Last was our accompanist.

The first Worstead Festival took place in this year, and Audrey and I with other artistes presented a recital in the Parish Church.

Sadly, George James died in this year and we attended his funeral service in the Cathedral. George had a fine bass voice, and in his retirement from professional singing involving performances with the English Opera Company, he had conducted quite a few operas for N.O.Ps. and had been a member of the cathedral choir.

We performed in an *Elijah* at St Mary's Baptist Church, Norwich, one of several occasions in which the St Mary's choir and the Sheringham and Cromer Choral Societies' choirs merged to give performances. On this occasion, the programme shows that we were also joined by the Princes Street Congregational choir and the Shakespeare Memorial Churches.

The Bartered Bride was Norfolk Opera Players' next production at the Theatre Royal, with the Norwich Ballet Club providing the dancing and the Costessey Secondary Modern School providing gymnasts. At this time, Costessey School had some gymnasts of national standing, and their contribution added tremendous zest to our production.

> Ballet and acrobats had made their mark,
> Giving another dimension to our stage:
> Small wonder then that we should now embark
> On work with which these factions could engage.
> Thus Bartered Bride by Smetana was chosen
> In which we joyously expressed ourselves,
> To bring our opera tally to a dozen
> (In days when counting still was done in twelves).

I organised a second Grand Charity Concert at the Theatre Royal, in aid of Audrey's Association. On this occasion contributors were Norfolk Opera Players, Norwich Ballet Club, Norwich Mozart Orchestra, Norwich Symphonic Wind, The Notre Dame School Choir and the Theatre Royal Drama Club. On this occasion, a small motorised boat was pulled on to the stage by the Norfolk Sea Scouts. This was donated by Pointers' Garage (now re-named?) and presented to the Association's Chairman, Mrs Lois Nickerson. The boat was to be raffled with tickets available at this concert, and throughout the ensuing year at sales and other venues. This was again the result of Audrey's extraordinary talent of cadging for charity I haven't a record of how much profit was made at the concert itself, but I do remember that there was a substantial audience.

This year finished as ever, with Maddermarket Music Hall.

Another gem in our own repertoire (I think it merits this description by dint of audience appreciation) was 'Gathering up shells from the shore', in which that activity was depicted, by three of the four, rhythmically and in concert, whilst the fourth created mayhem with his individual interpretation. No marks for guessing who that was. There were other pieces for the four of us, equally chaotic, with the long feather from Audrey's hat menacing my nostrils as she swayed to the rhythm.

Tuesday 21 October to Saturday 25 October

The Bartered Bride

Cast in order appearance

Jenik, son of Micha's first wife	**Alan Temple**
Marenka, daughter of Krusina and Ludmila	**Ann Youngman**
Kecal, the village marriage broker	**Robert Yates**
Krusina, a well-to-do peasant	**Jeremy Andrews**
Ludmila, his wife	**Sally Stock**
Vasek, son of Micha and Hata	**Peter Hudson**
Manager of a company of strolling players	**Sten Knudsen**
Esmerelda, dancer of that company	**Sheila Box**
Indian, a member of that company	**Maurice Grief**
Micha, a rich farmer	**Roy Emerson**
Hata, his wife	**Catherine Taylor**

CHORUS OF VILLAGERS
Caroline Bald, Vera Buckell, Carol Coombes, Margaret Dixon, Myra Francis, Yvonne Ireson, Hilary Jex, Sheila Kiggins, Janet King, June Martin, Juliet Norton, Janet Shreeve, Gwenneth Walker, Julia Yates, Audrey Yates, Percy Ash, Ken Davis, Harry Dawson, Paul England, David Green, Alan Griffiths, Maurice Grief, Eric Hartley, Sten Knudsen, Christopher Millett, Derek Smithson.

DANCERS
Janice Baker, Penny Cooke, Rosalind Delf, Jane Macdonald, Hazel Magnus, Julia Marcantonio, Joyce Mason, Linda Palmer, Eileen Pennington, Patricia Peter, Kay Pyett, Susan Read, Diane Taylor, Margaret Taylor, Sarah Sisley, Marigold Smith, Christopher Scales, George Wrzesien.

ACROBATS
Derek Leveridge, John Matthews, Adrian Barker, Andrew Barker, Philip Bush, Christopher Copage, Paul Francis, Richard Gilbert, Malcolm Gurney.

Catering Facilities. There are fully licensed bars in the stalls and circle for your convenience. Take advantage of our service to order your drinks for the interval. Popular prices. Coffee may be obtained through the circle bar.

The Bartered Bride **at the Theatre Royal**

89

Chapter 23 - 1970

Recital (Diss Church) ~ Concert (Maddermarket Theatre) ~ Concert
(Cromer Town Hall) ~ *Mikado* (concert version) (Pier Pavilion,
Lowestoft) ~ *The Gondoliers* (Cromer Pier Pavilion) ~ *Messiah*
(Heacham Church) ~ Wangford Festival *Mikado* (concert version)
(St Felix School Hall) ~ Recital (Trinity Presbyterian Church, Norwich)
~ Family Recital (South Lowestoft Methodist Church) ~ *Creation*
(St Mary's Baptist Church, Norwich) ~ Family Recital (St Remigius
Church, Hethersett) ~ *Otello* (concert version) (Triennial Festival,
Hippodrome Theatre, Great Yarmouth) ~ Concert incl. Bach's
Magnificat (Roman Catholic Cathedral, Norwich) ~ Concert (Princes
Street Congregational Church) ~ Christmas Music (inc. Schutz's
Christmas Story) (Town Hall, Great Yarmouth) ~ Haydn's *The Seasons*
(St Bennet's Church, Beccles) ~ Concert (Salvation Army Citadel,
Norwich) ~ Maddermarket Music Hall.

This year was to provide us with a full diary again, and perhaps it would be interesting to use this year's events as typical of the last twenty, with three recitals, five concerts, three concert versions of operatic works, one opera, five oratorios and about four 'Music Halls'. Our itinerary took us (in alphabetical order) to Beccles, Cromer, Diss, Great Yarmouth, Heacham, Hethersett, Lowestoft, Norwich and Wangford.

As for previous years, I will continue to remark on each presentation. As I have progressed with these memoirs, it has become increasingly a chronicle of local events, and of people involved in them.

The recital at Diss and the concert at the Maddermarket Theatre are recorded in the programme simply by a list of performers and of their contributions, with no dates given. The Maddermarket concert listed as performers Janet and John Bates, gifted members of Norwich Players, who contributed dramatic readings. Other performers were Sally Stock, Alan Temple, Rita Green, and Eileen Last, accompanist.

At the Diss concert, again with Eileen Last as pianist, Audrey and I were joined by singers Anthony Wick and Rita Green. John Last and our daughter Julia played movements from a Cimarosa concerto, and a Bach trio sonata. Readings were by Janet Bates.

A contingent of Norfolk Opera Players presented a concert at Cromer Town Hall. Included in the offerings was a monologue by Eric Hartley. I think this was his 'Sweeney Tod' piece, a masterful, bloodcurdling interpretation, performed in incomparable style, not only on this occasion, but in many a Maddermarket Music Hall performance.

Mikado at Lowestoft included Jane Manning, Sally Stock, Anthony Wicks, Audrey and myself and two artistes from Ipswich. This was when Jane arrived half an hour before the performance, flying directly from an engagement in Spain! She missed the rehearsal and Claude Richards had a deputy on standby!

Norfolk Opera Players in The Gondoliers

Sally Stock
(Tessa)

Nicolas Bloom
(Antonio)

Janet King
(Fiametta)

Jeremy Andrews
(Guiseppe)

Leslie Smith
(Luiz)

Audrey Yates
(The Duchess)

Jonathan Meddings
(Producer)

Ann Youngman
(Casilda)

Eric Hartley
(The Duke)

Alan Temple
(Marco)

Bridget Roper
(Gianetta)

Robert Yates
(Grand Inquisitor)

Hilary Jex
(Inez)

91

I had decided to go back to Cromer Pier with Norfolk Opera Players, in an effort to recoup money, which we were losing at the Theatre Royal. We re-launched ourselves with *The Gondoliers*. One of our members who lived in Cromer provided the men with a barrel of beer back-stage, and I cannot remember how many times this was renewed during the week. You may shudder at this unprofessional indulgence. At first I was tempted to lay down the law, but the fact is that having leniently allowed the first barrel to stay, I realised that they sang a darn sight better than when they remained thirsty. They were no mean drinkers. Surely the cachucha, fandango and bolero were never more energetically danced on any stage?

Financial matters could not be ignored,
And Cromer had been missed for many a day
So back we went, and thus we could afford
To lose at home, if we could win away.
Gondoliers came first, *Mikado* next,
Enriching our experience, and our treasury,
And thus with our financial muscles flexed
The flow of cash at home could be more leisurely.

Messiah at Heacham was in the company of Elizabeth Lawrence, soprano and Roland Smith, two singers with whom we had no previous association. Conductor was Wilfred Copesake again and the organist was Trevor Hughes. I have not made a study of how many *Messiah*s we performed with organ accompaniment and how many with orchestra. The latter were, of course, much more satisfying.

I think it was Marguerite Chilvers who asked me to sing the part either of the Mikado or Pooh-Bah (I can't remember which) in a concert version of that Gilbert and Sullivan Opera at the Wangford Festival. Professional baritone Norman Tattersall sang either Mikado or Pooh-Bah. Jane Manning also sang on that occasion in a performance of Haydn's *The Seasons*. (She had a streaming cold and kept a hot-water bottle in her lap!)

We were part of a double quartet of singers for the recital at the Trinity Presbyterian Church, in music ranging from that of Wilby and Tomkins of the sixteenth century to Bach and Pergolesi of the seventeenth and eighteenth centuries. Instrumentalists were Kenneth Ryder, harpsichord, Sarah Harper, flute, Margaret Crofts, violin, and Barry Wright, 'cello.

We presented another Family Recital at Lowestoft, with contributions also from David Woodrow (excellent trumpet player from the Salvation Army Band) and Alwyn Green (Rita Green's son, previously Salvation Army Band and now trombonist with the Bournemouth Symphony Orchestra). Elizabeth and Julia made contributions (readings and flute solos). Colin Goodchild played piano and organ, Charles Dickie (then a fellow student with Elizabeth at Colchester) played 'cello.

I sang in a performance of Haydn's *Creation* at St Mary's Baptist Church, celebrating fifty years service by Cyril Pearce as Organist and Choirmaster. Also in this year, though not documented, Audrey and I sang as guest artistes at a dinner given in his honour, in St Mary's Church Rooms.

We presented another Family Recital at Hethersett Church in October together with Rita Green, soprano, Arthur Andrews, trumpet, and Colin Goodchild, piano, and Charles Dickie. Julia, Lizzie and I performed 'Doc weichet ihr tollen' from Bach's Cantata No. 8, with Julia playing the flute obligatos and Lizzie at the piano.

Closely following George James's memorial service in the Cathedral came another for Steve Aymes, press music and drama critic, also a friend, who like George, was 'going too soon'. Later on, George Usher, another Press critic and a great supporter of local activities was to pass on. Others similarly involved have been Gordon Leach and Bill Coleman. Later on still came Charles Roberts, now officially retired as theatre critic, but nevertheless still active as occasional critic, author, actor, and producer. It is right that I should say here that in all our years of singing we have enjoyed great support and encouragement from all these men.

Perhaps this is the right moment to make mention of the several garden parties to entertain many friends, most of whom have been musical associates in some field or other, numbering a hundred or more, and on one occasion two hundred.

On these occasions, I have written a script for a send-up, for instance, of a Gardeners' Question Time, or an Antiques Road Show, or a psychiatrist's clinic. At the last of these events, Charles Roberts was question master at a Gardener's Question Time, and exercised considerable ingenuity in combating the ad-libbing of various contributors.

In the Norfolk and Norwich Triennial Festival, Antony Hopkins presented an unusual concert. It was the realisation of his long-felt ambition, in his words 'to put two great masterpieces *Othello* and *Otello* side by side, and see in the most vivid terms what a wonderful adaptation Boito, Verdi's librettist, made in a task which might have been daunting...the hardest decision has been what to leave out... To help me in my task, I shall have actors to present Shakespeare's text, a star-studded cast of singers and the City of Birmingham Symphony Orchestra, and the Norwich Festival Choir'. Well, I won't say that Audrey and I were included in the reference to a star-studded cast. Shall we say that we augmented it? Antony Hopkins had asked for us, Audrey to sing the part of Emilia, and I to sing the parts of Montano and Ludovico. Miriam Cannell, Festival Organiser, had first 'phoned Audrey to ask if she could sing a top A. The part of Emilia is in the mezzo range, but in the excerpt chosen an A was required. It was a great experience. We sang with Mary Wells (Desdemona) Ronald Dowd (Otello) and Bryan Drake (Iago), all operatic stars of the day. Their spoken counterparts were Sara Kestelman (Desdemona) Paul Rogers (Othello and Iago).

The Hippodrome is an amphitheatre, with tiered seats rising all round from a performing circle. The Birmingham Symphony Orchestra was positioned in the circle with us (the choir and soloists) on one side of the tiered circle and the actors on the opposite side. The rest of the seats were occupied by audience. The sound of the orchestra was superb. One can only hope that choir and soloists were worthy of that sound. We rehearsed in the afternoon somewhere in

Yarmouth (I can't remember where) and met the rest of the cast. They were all very pleasant and totally unassuming. The acoustics at the Hippodrome, with the Birmingham Symphony Orchestra playing from the centre circle were so good, that when listening to the equally splendid Bournemouth Symphony Orchestra playing in St Andrew's Hall during the Festival, the acoustical comparison was odious. Improvements to that establishment were about to take place, and in a chance meeting with the then City Architect, David Percival, I asked whether such improvements could be geared towards making the hall into a kind of amphitheatre. Lack of money, of course, precluded, and as I write, we are still stuck with St Andrew's Hall as the only concert hall in Norwich, a fine city.

Audrey and I contributed to a Bach's *Magnificat* in the Roman Catholic Cathedral, and had to combat, for the first time, the terrible acoustical properties. We were positioned under the tower with our voices no doubt ascending to heaven, but not reaching the congregation with any authority.

It is difficult to remember in detail all of the performances in which we were involved, but reference to the programmes certainly reminds us of the privilege we enjoyed in performing with so many talented musicians and singers. For instance, at a concert in the Lecture Hall of Princes Street Congregational Church, the orchestral players were Michael Butcher, flute, David Watering, clarinet, John McKenna, oboe and bassoon, Joan Roe, piano and Gladys King, piano.

Another name, that of John Roper, appears in the programme of a performance at Yarmouth Town Hall of *The Christmas Story* by Heinrich Schutz. John sang the tenor solos, and Beryl Mann was the soprano. John of course is extremely well known in Yarmouth, not only for his singing, but as a pianist and conductor.

The contralto voice is not catered for in *The Christmas Story*, neither is it in Haydn's *The Seasons* which was presented by the Beccles Choral Society, with Reginald Firth conducting and Colin Clouting leading the orchestra. Beccles was fortunate in being able to secure the services of Colin, leader then, and for many years after, of the Norwich Philharmonic Orchestra. Other soloists were Ann Youngman, soprano and Richard White, tenor. Ann, at this time, was a leading soprano with Norfolk Opera Players. Richard, of course, we had sung with on many an occasion, and would again in future concerts.

The programme of the concert at the Salvation Army Citadel reveals the names of several musicians and actors, well-known and respected, viz: Bandmaster John Gibson, Songsters leader, Beryl Mann and Rita Green (sopranos) David Woodrow (trumpet) Ian Emmerson and Jonathon Meddings (of Maddermarket fame). The concert was in aid of the Pakistan Disaster Appeal.

Maddermarket Music Hall concluded our year's musical engagement.

At the commencement of the academic year, our daughter Julia attended Dartington College of Music and The Arts, for tuition in flute playing. We at home commenced adding 800 square feet to our bungalow, in order to provide a music room, and other additional space.

Chapter 24 -1971

Messiah (High School Choral Society) (Town Hall, Great Yarmouth) ~ Come, Ye Sons of Art (Thorpe Grammar School) ~ *Elijah* (St John the Baptist Church, Harleston) ~ Haydn's *Nelson Mass* and Bach Cantata *Liebster Jesu, mein Verlangen* (Norwich Cathedral) ~ *Iolanthe* (concert version) (Pier Pavilion, Lowestoft) ~ *Mikado* (concert version) (Dereham Memorial Hall) ~ *Mikado* (Cromer Pier Pavilion) ~ *Merry Wives of Windsor* (Theatre Royal, Norwich) ~ *Fantasia on Christmas Carols* and Gordon Jacob's *Highways* (Beccles Church) ~ *Messiah* (Old Grammar School Hall, Stowmarket) ~ Maddermarket Music Hall.

A *Messiah* to which I contributed at Great Yarmouth is memorable for more than its musical content. It was a performance by the Great Yarmouth High School Choral Society, conducted by John Roper, who was 'musical director at the High School and founder of the two-year old choral society', to quote the Press critique. At the final flourish of the baton (of which there had been many, because John was more than somewhat outgoing in his conducting,) John proclaimed a 'Bless you' to the choir, and they responded with the sort of adulation accorded to a pop-star, with screams from the girls and more muted expressions of delight from the boys. This was certainly a 'one-off' *Messiah*.

The tenor on that occasion was David Clark, a Norwich parson with whom we had sung on other occasions, and who is now living somewhere in the Midlands.

I sang with the Thorpe Choral Society and the Blofield Choral Society in a performance of Purcell's *Come Ye Sons of Art* at Thorpe Grammar School. These choirs augmented the school choir, and the school orchestra was also augmented by one or two professionals. Two school pupils, Patricia Arnold, soprano, and Stephen Gowland, counter-tenor, were the other soloists. The concert included orchestral items, with solo contributions from Marion Adcock, Anita Smart, Jane Bardwell and Carolyn Adcock.

The performance of Mendelssohn's *Elijah* at St. John the Baptist Church, Harleston was 'in celebration of the centenary of the opening of the Church'. Audrey must have been busy because she had arranged that proceeds should be in aid of the Norfolk Association for the Disabled (this last word having now replaced the word Handicapped). Lowestoft Choral Society had been recruited, with their conductor Claude Richards and accompanist Marianne Long. The piano had been loaned by A.W.Cooke & Son (no doubt through Audrey's and my acquaintance with Arthur Cooke).

The Students' Music Society of the U.E.A. invited Audrey and me to contribute to a presentation of Haydn's *Nelson Mass* at the Cathedral. I was also to sing the bass aria, and a duet with Anne Bartlett, soprano, in a Bach cantata *Liebster Jesu, mein Verlangen*. Accompaniments to both works were by the 'Orchestra Ecclesia' led by Paul Clarke, and other instrumentalists in the cantata were Barry Wright, cello and Stephen Westrup, organ continuo. Until this year, Stephen Westrup was a very successful chorus master of LSO chorus!

At the concert performance of *Iolanthe* at Lowestoft, other soloists included Sally Stock and Brian Tuffrey.

The concert at Dereham Memorial Hall by the Mid-Norfolk Choral Society, consisted of a performance of *Hiawatha's Wedding Feast* with Peter Pease singing the tenor solo, and of *The Mikado* in which Audrey and I were singing with Sylvia Foxwell, Donald MacKenzie, David Johnson, Mary Brown and Ruby Twaite. The accompanist was Rosamunde Evans, the conductor Colin Goodchild, who had taken over from our old friend Edwin Kennedy, who had moved away. Another old friend, Norman Abbot, was narrator.

The *Mikado* at Cromer Pier Pavilion was produced by Peter Spalding, who was drama tutor at Keswick College. Peter had produced *The Deal* at the Maddermarket Theatre for Norfolk Opera Players, so I decided to let him have a go at producing a Gilbert and Sullivan opera. A producer of experience in any sphere has no problems with Gilbert and Sullivan if they follow Bridget D'Oyly Carte's 'prompt copy', which details every move. Nowadays, producers are inclined to be innovative, with local or topical innuendoes 'embellishing' the work of W. S. Gilbert. Some are successful, others are not. I think that *Mikado*, though not exactly in the mode of Bridget D'OylyCarte, went reasonably well, with Eric Hartley helping Peter in infusing some traditional G. & S. into the performance. Perhaps also the back-stage lubrication again assisted. Certainly the Gentleman of Japan could never have been more effusive.

Daughter Julia, having finished her year's flute course at Dartington, started a saxophone course at Leeds, eventually playing both alto and tenor saxophone in various professional bands.

Notable in this year was our production of *The Merry Wives of Windsor* at the Theatre Royal. Notable because of it being conducted by Antony Hopkins. I had asked Antony (yes, we were on Christian name terms) to conduct, because I knew that he had been superseded in his post of conductor of the Norwich Philharmonic Orchestra by Philip Ledger and Brian Runnett, and sensed that he would like to keep his Norwich connections alive. I remember his referring to the Theatre orchestra pit after £14,000 had been spent by the City Council on various improvements and re-furbishing, as 'the deepest pit in captivity'. In those days, Norfolk Opera Players received enormous press coverage, and because of Antony Hopkins' presence, coverage extended to a television interview. Jonathon Meddings produced the opera and Emyr Evans had been responsible for the musical preparation. Julia played in the orchestra.

> The choice of Theatre shows does e'er perplex
> Needing the judgement of Solomon to solve
> Whereas the only aids we can annex
> Are musical appetite and firm resolve.
> The *Merry Wives* had pleased in '64,
> On tiny stage, with not too many voices,
> So what was wrong with giving an encore

With greater vocal and orchestral noises?
Thus to the Theatre now reconstituted
With Tony Hopkins flourishing the baton
From deepest pit yet known (it was reputed)
And scarcely in view no matter what he sat on.

It was about this time that Roy Emerson, who played Dr Caius in *The Merry Wives*, initiated a venture, which he entitled 'The Thursday Club'. Its aims were to encourage a wider understanding of all aspects of the production and performance of opera, and to provide a forum for discussion and general socialising. It met, as its name implies on Thursdays at Wensum Lodge, usually in the undercroft, which now houses Jurnet's Bar.

An ambitious start was made with a talk by Douglas Robinson, then Chorus Master of the Royal Opera. A particular strength of Norfolk Opera Players at that time was its chorus, and it was of value to have demonstrated the importance of good chorus work in a production.

By courtesy of
Eastern
Counties
Newspapers

The Merry Wives of Windsor
Mistress Ford (Ann Youngman) and Mistress Page (Audrey Yates)

There were a number of other speakers, all of local or national renown, including Roy himself who lectured on the works of Wagner. The club made one or two excursions, one of them to see La Belle Hélène in Cambridge, and another to the Covent Garden Opera House, where we watched a rehearsal of *Wozzeck* with Geraint Evans singing and Colin Davies conducting.

Unfortunately, the enterprise came to a relatively speedy demise due to Roy's increased pressure of work as a professor at the University of East Anglia. Roy's wife Audrey later became Norfolk Opera Players Secretary, a job that she performed with great distinction.

The concert at Beccles included Vaughan Williams' *Fantasia on Christmas Carols*, in which I enjoyed singing the baritone solos once again. Also in the programme was *Highways*, a cantata of travel by Gordon Jacob. This also contained baritone solos. I can remember nothing of this work.

I think it was Richard White who asked me to join him and two lady singers in a performance of *Messiah* at Stowmarket. I remember that for piano continuo, the pianist had put drawing pins in the hammer felts, so that a harpsichord effect was produced – very ingenious.

Again we performed in Maddermarket Music Hall. Perhaps I ought to give some atmosphere to my annual reference to these events. Our repertoire was not extensive, simply because our 'Aspidistras' act seemed to bear repetition. It was of course, a send-up of Victorian songs, which we arranged as duets. In Tosti's 'Parted', as I have said, we got into terrible tangles whilst passionately declaring our love for each other. 'You must go back to your life, I must go back to mine' – very difficult, with each of us hanging on. 'Come into the Garden Maud' commenced with Audrey reading poetry on stage and I standing behind a trellis. My protestations never bore fruit, because when I tried to join her, she had gone, and a whole cycle of appearances and disappearances ensued, leaving me bereft.

This is, perhaps, the opportunity to pay tribute to those two men who 'ran' the Maddermarket Theatre so successfully, for so many years, Ian Emmerson and Jonathon Meddings. Their ingenuity and humour in coaching us for our 'Aspidistra' duets and 'Glee Singers' quartets made rehearsals and performances a happy experience.

Chapter 25 - 1972

Concert (Town Hall, Great Yarmouth) ~ *H.M.S. Pinafore* and *Not in Front of the Waiter* (Cromer Pier Pavilion) ~ Family Recital (St Nicholas Church, Dersingham) ~ *Tyndale* (Cromer Parish Church) ~ Haydn's *Nelson Mass* (Norwich School Musical Society, Norwich Cathedral) ~ *The Creation* (King's College Chapel, Cambridge) ~ Christmas Music (inc. *The New Born King*) (Central Hall, Deneside, Great Yarmouth) ~ Bach's *Christmas Oratorio* (Norwich High School and Norwich School, Norwich Cathedral) ~ Maddermarket Music Hall.

Rita Green, Richard White, Audrey and I were joined by David Woodrow (trumpet) and Colin Goodchild (piano) at Great Yarmouth Town Hall, in a concert in aid of funds for the Great Yarmouth Barnardo's Helpers' League.

In listing this concert, one of many in which Audrey and I were involved at Yarmouth, it is not easy to remember the detail of the evening's performance. However, the programme shows that we performed quartets and duets in addition to solo items, my contribution including the blood curdling 'Edward' by Loewe. I often wonder what effect this piece had on an audience, with the dastardly story unfolding with piteous groans punctuating the singing. Colin Goodchild (as well as accompanying us) played a Schubert Impromptu, and David Woodrow played two movements from Haydn's trumpet concerto, and two other pieces.

Writing this now, I must again bemoan the fact that the concert hall within the Town Hall is no longer used for concerts. It was so excellent as a concert venue for both performers and audience.

H.M.S. Pinafore at Cromer Pier Pavilion was produced by Margot Warne, and conducted by Colin Goodchild. Colin's name has appeared in quite a few of my musical recollections of earlier years but up to now I have said little of Margot Warne. Margot trained as a ballet dancer and pianist, and in this dual role in later years she founded and ran the Norwich Ballet Club. By this time I had invited her, with her dancers, to become affiliated to Norfolk Opera Players. When choosing operas for future performances, we would endeavour to select those, which involved ballet or dancing. With knowledge already gained of N.O.P. performances, we invited her to produce *H.M.S. Pinafore*. She was more than equal to the task, and I am sure that the crew danced an impeccable hornpipe.

H.M.S. Pinafore is not a long opera, so we presented a double bill with *Not in Front of the Waiter*, a small opera by Offenbach. You will have seen how many times Eileen Last's name has appeared in these memoirs. In addition to the performances listed to date in which she was involved, she was also rehearsal pianist for N.O.Ps. *Not in Front of the Waiter* gave her an opportunity to extend her talent to conducting. Edward Barnell produced. 'Barney', as we knew him, was a great Gilbert and Sullivan man, and both Audrey and I had worked under his supervision as producer on other occasions.

I think the double bill went well.

Back to the pier with *Not in Front of the Waiter*
And *Pinafore* appropriately following
The former being served as titillator
The latter just as easy in the swallowing.

We presented another Family Recital at St Nicholas Church, Dersingham.
Our daughter Elizabeth Yates (piano and readings) recruited David Humpage
(violin), Charles Dickie ('cello), Stephanie Nunn (oboe), Susan Humpage
(soprano), and Julia Yates (flute). Audrey and I also contributed and Colin
Goodchild was our accompanist. The performers, other than the Yates family
and Colin, were all music students with Lizzie at Colchester. Elizabeth, Julia and
I were together again in the Bach cantata *Doch weichet ihr tollen vergeblichen
Sorgen* This concert was obviously part of the local Flower Festival, since
(quoting) 'during the interval the audience is invited to look around at the Floral
Arrangements'.

By courtesy of Eastern Counties Newspapers

The *Nelson Mass* by Haydn introduced me to Catherine Lawson, who sang the contralto part in this work. We were later to know her more closely, because she became Audrey's singing teacher. Catherine was ex-English Opera, and married to Steve Waters, professional clarinettist. Other performers were Katherine Morgan, soprano, and David Clark, tenor. Having lost one half of this programme I have no recollection of who accompanied or who conducted, but the performance was for the Norwich School Musical Society.

Eileen Last was the conductor in a performance by the Hewett School Senior Choir, of Part I of Haydn's *Creation* at King's College Chapel, Cambridge. The soloists were Rita Green, Richard White and myself. The organist was none other than David Willcocks, a charming man who showed us around the college during the interval between afternoon rehearsal and evening performance. The Choir sang other items, in which they were joined by members of staff, parents and friends.

Later in this year I was again at Yarmouth (Central Hall, Deneside on this occasion). I think mine was a substantial contribution to the programme, because I was baritone soloist in *The New Born King* by Gordon Jacob and *Fantasia on Christmas Carols* by Vaughan Williams. I also contributed songs. Back in 1967, I had sung in the Gordon Jacob work with the Yarmouth Society, but again I can't remember anything about it. Presumably I would if confronted with a score. The accompanist on this occasion was Margaret Gee, and the conductor Gregory Underwood.

The *Christmas Oratorio* in the Cathedral was again with Catherine Waters (Catherine Lawson now using her married name) Kate Morgan and David Clark. The choir and orchestra were of the combined Norwich High School and Norwich School. The programme doesn't mention the conductor, but I am sure that this was Pat Clouting.

Of course, Maddermarket Music Hall concluded the year's musical diary. Having given a little information on the content of The Aspidistras' performance in last year's diary of events I will tell you a little of another contribution to the yearly event. In a performance of 'Pale Hands I Love' (one of the Indian love lyrics), Audrey nursed an injured finger, and my attempt to add physical reinforcement to the words by clasping her hands, presented me with considerable difficulty.

Chapter 26 - 1973

Messiah (St Alban's Church, Lakenham) ~ *Carmen* (Theatre Royal, Norwich) ~Family Recital (St Michael's Church, Aylsham) ~ Concert (Connaught Hall, Attleborough) ~ Recital (St Michael's Church, Aylsham) ~ *Creation* (St Mary the Virgin Church, Heacham) ~ Family Recital (Worstead Church) ~ *Dido & Aeneas* (concert version) (St Margaret's Church, Cley and Assembly House, Norwich) ~ Recital (St Margaret's Church, Cley) ~ *The Marriage* and *The Sorcerer* (Cromer Pier Pavilion) ~ *Messiah* (St Mary the Virgin Church, Heacham) ~ Gilbert & Sullivan evening (Town Hall, Hunstanton and Guildhall of St George, King's Lynn) ~ Maddermarket Music Hall

The year's performances commenced with Parts I & II of the *Messiah* at St Alban's Church, Lakenham, presented by the Norwich City College Singers and Orchestra (leader Eric Burdett), and conducted by Howard Burrell. This was one of the few occasions on which I sang the rarely performed second part of 'The Trumpet Shall Sound', responding to the 'Da Capo'.

The other soloists must have been students at the Norwich City College, for an inspection of the programme reveals unfamiliar names, excepting perhaps for Alan Green.

In April, Norfolk Opera Players presented Bizet's *Carmen* at the Theatre Royal, marking a decade of N.O.P. performances during which time we had presented sixteen operas, large and small.

As I have remarked before, we did enjoy substantial press coverage in those days, and I have an article occupying a full sheet (large in those days) of the *Eastern Daily Press* of April 3rd, written by our old friend Charles Roberts (then fairly new to this area), publicising the event, with photographs, and recounting the history of Norfolk Opera Players.

The photographs in the theatre programme however, were a trifle disorientated. I was shown as Arthur Cooke, Arthur was shown as Robert Arnett and Robert Arnett was shown as Robert Yates. We decided to stick to our allotted roles, which were: -

> Escamillo - Robert Yates.
> Remendado - Arthur Cooke.
> A Guide - Robert Arnett.

Sally Stock, correctly depicted in the programme, played Carmen. We had recruited quite a number of newcomers for this opera and Robert Arnett was one of them. In later presentations he was to take more major roles. Norwich Ballet Club provided the dancers, under the direction of Margot Warne and the Norwich Boys' Choir, cast as street urchins, rehearsed under the musical direction of Kenneth Ryder, Jack Evans and Rosemary Kimmins. The list of boys included the name of Justin Fashanu, later to become a star footballer. He and his brother John were adopted by the parents of the professional mezzo-soprano Susan Anderson. Altogether there were 109 performers with an orchestra of 40 players led by Michael Badminton and conducted by Emyr Evans.

The opera was produced by Richard White, with whom we had sung in many an oratorio. His appointment in this capacity resulted from a conversation he and I had when travelling back from King's College, Cambridge, in September 1972. Richard said that, since graduating he had developed more interest in producing opera than he had in singing. While at university he had in fact gained much experience in this activity. With our policy of ringing the changes in our selection of producers and musical directors, I persuaded the Norfolk Opera Players committee to engage Richard as producer for our presentation of *Carmen*.

**Founder members of the Norfolk Opera Players rehearsing for *Carmen*
Left to right: M.E.Grief, Ann Youngman, Paul England, Bridget Roper,
Robert and Audrey Yates, with Eileen Last at the piano**

Carmen is an opéra-comique with a tragic story and a tragic ending. We received a bomb warning on the first night, and evacuated the audience. It was a hoax, and happily the tragic ending was restricted to stage only.

> Thus we came to nineteen seventy-three,
> Marking a full decade of joys and vigours,
> And so proclaimed an anniversary
> Of N.O.P.s attaining double figures.
> *Carmen* was chosen for this proud occasion,
> And Norwich boys were singing in our ranks,
> And they and we enhanced our reputation,
> Not only with the crowd, but at the bank.
> And notwithstanding some intimidation
> From telephonic warning diabolical
> *Carmen* lived up to every expectation
> And the bang with which it went was metaphorical.

Yet another Family Recital, this time in Aylsham Church. Not just family of course, because it included three of Lizzie's college friends, Stephanie Nunn, oboe, Kim Lewis Lavender, readings and Charles Dickie, 'cello. Lizzie was now listed as Elizabeth Dickie, since the knot had been tied. Unfortunately it was not to last long, a matter of some regret. Eileen Last again accompanied our songs excepting for Bach's 'Doch weichet, lhr tollen' to which Elizabeth and Julia contributed.

I know that Audrey and I sang at a concert during Attleborough Carnival week in June. I think we were asked at a fairly late date, by a friend with whom I used to work, Ken Abel, possibly to replace some other failed contribution. I do remember that our choice of songs was not appropriate to the occasion – 'too classical'. One learns!

I performed again at Aylsham, St Michael's Church, at the invitation of Howard Rooke (quite a force in later years, if not then, in Norfolk music). Other performers were Margaret Anderson, soprano, Katherine Wilkinson, contralto, Richard Stanley, oboe, resident clergyman Jack Vyse, readings, Howard himself and his wife Elizabeth Rooke, each playing organ.

Rita Green, Richard White and I sang in a performance of the *Creation* at Heacham church. The organist was Brian Ellum, the orchestra leader Susan Price and the conductor Wilfred Copestake.

The recital at Worstead Church was 'family' plus Colin Goodchild, piano, accompanying many of the contributions.

In July, Audrey joined Penelope Mackay and Alison Humphreys, sopranos, Michael Goldthope, tenor, and Michael Allard, harpsichord in a concert performance of Purcell's *Dido and Aeneas* at St Margaret's Church, Cley.

In August, we were back at Cley for a recital of songs in which we were joined by Doris Levett, solo piano, and Patrick King accompanying us.

Norfolk Opera Players performed *The Marriage* by Martinu and *The Sorcerer* by Gilbert and Sullivan at Cromer Pier. *The Marriage* is a delightfully humorous small opera, and one that I remember with great affection. The story is by Gogol. A Russian local government officer is extremely shy, but is persuaded by a marriage broker to present himself, with others, in competition for the hand of a most eligible lady. I think that in our performance at the Maddermarket Theatre in 1965, I enjoyed playing the role of the shy local government officer as much as any other operatic role. Richard, however, decided to change the venue from 19th century St Petersburgh to a 21st century space station. I think, and I believe the audience did too, that he should have stuck to planet earth.

We then produced our pier show in September because our Theatre date had been postponed. *The Sorcerer* went well as I remember, but *The Marriage* was, I think, unconsummated. The other memory I have is of partnering Gladys Mallyon in the chorus of *The Sorcerer*, and swinging her off her feet in one of the rumbustious choruses. Gladys was mightily surprised and, I think, gratified - she was not a small lady.

Rita Green, Richard White, Audrey and I sang in the *Messiah* at Heacham Church, in December. It was this performance that convinced us that this was the coldest church in the county. All of our church performances of oratorio were preceded by afternoon rehearsal, and it was quite usual for soloists to be summoned to attend at 3 p.m., only to be obliged to sit through a long chorus rehearsal, ultimately to rehearse at about 5 p.m. I think that Heacham was no exception, and that the church was no warmer in the evening than in the afternoon.

The four of us stopped for a drink in Docking on the way back, and it was in the pub that Audrey said that we should at some time present a staged version of Mendelssohn's *Elijah*, an ambition which Richard had often voiced. Margot Warne had often mentioned that she had attended such a performance in the Albert Hall. We did achieve such a presentation, as you will read later.

I was invited by the West Norfolk Gilbert and Sullivan Operatic Society to join them in two concert performances of excerpts from several Gilbert and Sullivan operas. I remember suggesting that Kathleen Chapman should sing the soprano solos, which was agreed. Meeting Kathleen recently, she referred to the King's Lynn occasion. She said that she was so stricken with nerves beforehand that she lost her voice. She didn't dare tell me, but fortunately her voice returned in sufficient time for her to make a splendid contribution. I'm sure therefore that she enjoyed the concerts, which were at the Guildhall of St George, King's Lynn and the Town Hall Theatre, Hunstanton. The accompanist was Ann Pratt, and the orchestra was conducted by Wilfred Copestake.

The reader will probably get fed up with mention of Maddermarket Music Hall, but bear up, for there are quite a few more years to record, including this one.

Chapter 27 - 1974

Sleepers Wake and *Messe Solennelle* (St Benet's Church, Beccles) ~
Messiah (Fakenham Parish Church) ~ *Crucifixion* (St John's Church,
Bury St Edmunds) ~ Recital (Thurne Methodist Church) ~ Morning
Service for the Handicapped (Vauxhall Centre, Norwich) ~
Merrie England (concert version) (Town Hall, Great Yarmouth) ~
The Creation (Hewett School, Norwich) ~ Songs of Praise (Norwich
Cathedral) ~ Recital (Aylsham Methodist Church) ~
Merrie England (Cromer Pier Pavilion) ~ *Merrie England* (concert
version) (College of Further Education, Lowestoft) ~ *Dido & Aneas*
(concert version) (Assembly House, Norwich) ~ *Faust* (Theatre Royal,
Norwich) ~ *Messiah* (Garland Street Baptist Church, Bury St Edmunds)

We were certainly very busy in April, May and June of this year. I will give dates
of performances to illustrate.

6th April *Sleepers Wake* (Bach) and *Messe Solennelle* (Gounod) involved Rita
Green, John Roper and myself as soloists, with John Hammond at the organ, and
Reginald Firth conducting.

7th April *Messiah* at Fakenham Parish Church, orchestra lead by John
Winsworth, and conducted by Bill Purchase. Eileen Last provided harpsichord
continuo. Mention of the orchestra reminds me of the fact that, on the many
occasions that we sang with orchestras, familiar faces would appear in their
midst, due of course to the fact that almost invariably they were *ad hoc*, recruited
from the best musicians around.

12th April Richard White asked me to sing in Stainer's *Crucifixion* at Bury
St Edmunds, and only to please Richard, did I agree because I had long since
declared that enough was enough with this work. (My records do not reveal how
many performances, because programmes were never produced for such
occasions). Ultimately, I regretted having sung in this one, since it was a set fee,
which I never received. Here I should explain that for many years Audrey and I
had sung as semi-professionals, although we gave many charitable performances.

Easter Monday (has anyone got a 1974 diary?) This was the first of several
appearances at Thurne Methodist Church, requested by Clifford Cooke, farmer,
and then a patron of Norfolk Opera Players. His daughter Vera, now well known
in Norfolk and beyond as a gifted mezzo- soprano soloist, sang with Audrey and
me, together with Alan Parrott, tenor, David Osborne, guitar, and the Church
Sunday School choir.

2nd May. We sang in the concert hall of the Vauxhall Centre, Johnson
place, Norwich at a morning service conducted by the Right Reverend Aubrey
Aitken, the Bishop of Lynn. He had been a very good singer and he and I had
both entered the Norwich Competitive Festival some years earlier, both singing
'Why do the Nations' from Handel's *Messiah*. He mentioned this fact during the
service. Most sadly he spoke on this occasion with the aid of electronic

equipment following a vocal chord operation. He was a most likeable man, and I was to meet him again in a later year.

8th May. In a concert performance of Edward German's *Merrie England* at Great Yarmouth, Judy Reid was to sing the part of Jill-All-Alone, and Audrey the part of Queen Elizabeth. Unfortunately Judy was injured (happily, not too badly) in a car accident en route for the Town Hall. Audrey sang the two roles until Judy arrived, head bandaged, and with great stoicism sang her role for the rest of the performance. Other soloists were John Roper and Rita Green.

11th May. The performance of Haydn's *Creation* at the Hewett School was by the combined choirs of the St Peter's and Calvert Street Methodist churches, organised by the Norwich Festival Committee. They were conducted by Emyr Evans. The other soloists were Rita Green and David Clark. The programme makes no mention of orchestra, or accompanist. The admission charges were adult 30p Student/OAP 15p.

20th May. Mrs Ethel Tipple O.B.E., J.P. was chairman of the Norfolk Old People's Welfare Association and Audrey had worked with her, setting up a Day Centre for the Handicapped in Aylsham similar to one that Mrs Tipple had provided for the elderly. This association led Mrs Tipple to ask Audrey to sing at a 'Songs of Praise' service for the elderly at the Cathedral. She sang from the organ loft, accompanied by Michael Nicholas, then the cathedral organist.

15th June. We both sang at Aylsham Methodist Church in a concert organised by Les and Gladys Mallyon (both N.O.P. members). Maurice Grief, another N.O.P., chaired the concert. Maurice was the father of Ann and Bridget, two outstanding singers and performers in many of our productions. Maurice was a farmer, Methodist lay preacher, and possessor of an incredible voice of a tremendous range, which, if harnessed, would have brought stardom. But to Maurice, singing was a sideline. He had other hobbies too.

22nd to 29th June. *Merrie England* at Cromer Pier Pavilion was to be our last performance there. We had switched from Gilbert and Sullivan performances at Cromer, which had helped to balance the books, because of the plethora of G. & S. operas now being presented by other companies throughout the county.

We made a good job of *Merrie England*, but it did not have the box-office appeal of the G. & S operas. Audrey made an excellent Queen Elizabeth, and remembers the experience of being carried aloft on a litter by four men of the cast, good men and true, but not averse to an occasional shake of the litter.

> Nothing daunted, we went again in June
> With *Merrie England*, cloaked in all its splendour,
> But though we 'sold' each cameo and tune
> We rated pretty low as ticket vendor.

The other big event of this year was our production of Gounod's *Faust* at the Theatre Royal. To avoid paying the heavy royalties attached to the use of editions whose copyrights were held by the publishers, we decided to use a

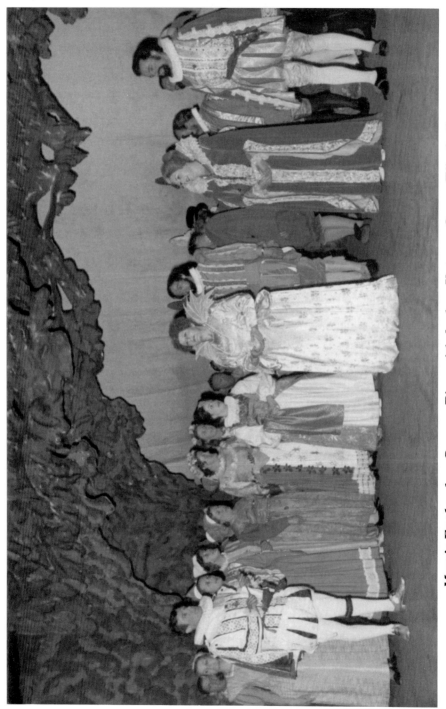

Merrie England on Cromer Pier, with Audrey Yates as Queen Elizabeth, Brian Tuffrey (right) as Sir Walter Raleigh, Kathleen Chapman as Bessie Throckmorton, and Phillip Chapman (left) as the Earl of Essex

translation by Emeritus Professor Proctor-Gregg, (who lived by the side of Lake Windermere).

I would need to study my old N.O.P. files to remind myself of how I came to hear of Professor Gregg. Anyway, he was a very distinguished music critic and had translated many operas. We invited him down and he stayed with Roy and Audrey Emerson, who threw a little party in his honour. Roy sang with Norfolk Opera Players and Audrey was Secretary and excellent as such. Roy too was a University of East Anglia professor, so he was on firm ground in his entertaining.

I took the part of Mephistopheles. When treading the boards before curtain up, which I always did, so as to familiarise myself with entrances and exits, Jack Bowhill, the Theatre's stage manager, passed by. I was so thoroughly disguised I thought that I was totally unrecognisable; I hadn't allowed for the taciturn Jack's perspicacity. Looking at something in the far distance he passed and said 'Hello Bob'.

Back stage after the show we met Jessie Griffiths, then Lady Mayoress and also the Chairman (note the title) of the Anguish Educational Trust. Eric Hartley introduced us and after explaining the financial plight of N.O.Ps, Jessie arranged for us to receive £2,000 grant from her organisation. This was our salvation, although we could no longer risk taking further operas to The Theatre Royal. At Dick Condon's request we did however take *The Mikado* and *The Yeomen of the Guard* there in the summer of 1975, although those shows did little to replenish our coffers.

Over our ten years at the Theatre Royal we had presented mostly those operas, which would not otherwise have been seen in this region. To my knowledge no other company had attempted such an undertaking, but exhortations to Dick Condon over the years had not resulted in reduced charges for our use of the Theatre. He was of course concerned with the Theatre's financial as well as artistic prowess. We enjoyed our years there and had an excellent rapport with Dick and with Jack Bowhill and his back-stage staff.

Audrey performed in a concert version of *Dido and Aeneas* at the Assembly House. The part of Aeneas was taken by John Aplin, who was later to earn great repute for his directorship of the Keswick Choir.

This year heralded the first of three oratorio performances to which we contributed at Garland Street Baptist Church in Ipswich. *Messiah* was chosen for this year.

Of course, the year ended with Maddermarket Music Hall. I should mention that, to some people, our singing activities were encapsulated in our Maddermarket performances, they having no knowledge of our more serious music.

Chapter 28 - 1975

Brahms' *Requiem* and Bach's *Sleeper's Wake* (St Peters Church, Kirkley, Lowestoft) ~ *The Creation* (Fakenham Parish Church) ~ Haydn's *Nelson Mass* (St Benet's Church, Beccles) ~ Recital (Thurne Methodist Church) ~ Mozart's *Requiem* (St Peter Mancroft, Norwich and Hingham Church) ~ Haydn's *Nelson Mass* and Buxtehude's *Jesu, Joy & Treasure* (St John's Church, Woodbridge) ~ Songs of Praise (Norwich Cathedral) ~ *The Mikado* and *Yeomen of the Guard* (Theatre Royal, Norwich) ~ *Elijah* (Garland Street Baptist Church, Bury St Edmunds) ~ Maddermarket Music Hall

We sang in many places in Lowestoft. On this occasion St Peter's Church, Kirkley, was the venue and the only other soloist was Rita Green, since Brahm's *Requiem* and Bach's *Sleepers, Wake!* involve only baritone and soprano soloists. This was a Lowestoft Choral Society presentation, with accompanists Marriane Long, piano, George Marley, organ and Victor Guy, oboe. The conductor was Christopher Prettyman.

Apart from being a magnificent choral work, Brahm's *Requiem* contains some wonderful moments for the two solo voices. *Sleepers, Wake!* includes two splendid duets for soprano and baritone. I have no doubt that we were entertained during the interval between afternoon rehearsal and evening performance by our old friends Roland and Winifred.

Creation with the Fakenham Choral Society again called for no solo contralto contribution. The two other soloists were Rita Green and Richard White.

Beccles Choral Society decided to promote one of their choir members, Audrey Mitchell, to sing the contralto role in Haydn's *Nelson Mass*. Needless to say, Rita Green and Richard White were there, as was Colin Clouting leading the orchestra, and Reginald Firth conductor.

We were at Thurne again on Easter Monday. This time the concert was chaired by Robert (Bob) Richardson. ('Robert' always looked more dignified on a programme I believed).

Vera Cooke, Audrey and I provided the singing, and daughter Julia provided a flute solo and the obligato to the Bach aria 'Doch weicht ihr tollen'. Accompanists were Mary Cooke (Vera's mother) and Colin Goodchild. The Revd Fred Pratt Green ('The Elocution Lesson') Nicholas Ireland (Piano solos) and Colin Riches ('The Resurrection' – Norfolk Style) also contributed.

The old firm (I'm not going to repeat the names yet again) were in action at St Peter Mancroft on 19th April with Mozart's *Requiem Mass* presented by Norwich Singers and conducted by Dennis Johnson with Kenneth Ryder, organist. Then on 23rd April it was repeated at St Andrew's Church, Hingham.

Our old friend Gordon Hawkins dug us out again for a performance of Haydn's *Nelson Mass* and Buxtehude's *Jesu, Joy and Treasure*. I cannot remember anything about this latter work, although the programme shows that it contains a bass solo. *Nelson Mass* of course was something we could now almost sing from memory. These works were with the Woodbridge Choral Society, conducted by Gordon Hawkins.

It was my turn to sing in the Norfolk Old People's Welfare Association concert at the Cathedral. It was my first meeting with Michael Nicholas who accompanied me (singing from the organ loft) in singing 'Lord God of Abraham' from Mendelssohn's *Elijah*.

As I have said before, the following for amateur Grand Opera was not sufficient to sustain performances at the Theatre Royal. My approaches to Dick Condon, then theatre manager, to reduce the hiring costs, met with no success. However, he had suggested that we might make some money if we presented a Gilbert and Sullivan opera in May. (I think he really wanted to complete his summer programme).

We decided to present *The Mikado* on Tuesday and Friday (20th and 23rd May) and *The Yeomen of the Guard* on Wednesday, Thursday and Saturday (21st, 22nd and 24th May). I played the title part in *The Mikado* and Audrey played Katisha. She also played Dame Carruthers in *The Yeomen of the Guard*. Colin Goodchild conducted *The Mikado* and Chris Prettyman conducted *Yeomen*.

> We then prepared for June of '75
> With *Yeomen of the Guard* and the *Mikado*
> And showed how vigorously we thrive
> In spite of falling short of El Dorado.

This time I shall say 'the old quartet' instead of 'the old firm', but here we are again at Bury St Edmunds with John Ince at the organ and a choir and orchestra led by Ronald Ely and conducted by Ethelbert Taylor.

Music Hall completed the year's vocal activities once again. One of our Aspidistra acts 'revealed' Audrey as a lady of the harem (suitably unclad) and myself as a Sheik, with most of the singing coming from inside a tent!

The Yeomen of the Guard

111

Chapter 29 - 1976

Tales of Hoffman (St Andrew's Hall, Norwich) ~ Brahms' *Requiem*
(Fakenham Parish Church) ~ *Messiah* from Scratch (Cromer Church)
The Creation (Dereham Festival, Dereham Boys' School) ~ *Messiah*
(St Mary's Baptist Church, Norwich) ~ *Noye's Fludde* (Notre Dame High
School and St John's Catholic Cathedral, Norwich) *TheCreation*
(Tacket Street United Reformed Church, Ipswich) *Rich Man, Poor Man*
(Triennial Festival, Theatre Royal, Norwich) ~ Come into the Parlour
(Assembly House, Norwich) *Messiah* (Thorpe School) ~
Maddermarket Music Hall.

At a chance meeting with Bob Brister, who was then Leisure Officer with
Norwich City Council, he suggested that Norfolk Opera Players should present a
concert at St Andrew's Hall, possibly an oratorio. In the light of our
impecuniosity, stemming from the high cost of performing at the Theatre Royal,
I said that we could do more; we could bring opera there.

So it was that we presented tales of Hoffman at St Andrew's Hall in 1976.
Much work had to be done in altering levels, providing an apron, building a set,
additional lighting etc. I think, therefore, that this is the moment, in these
memoirs, to pay tribute to all those splendid people who work 'behind the
scenes' in the operatic productions. First, let me reproduce the final verses of my
eulogising couplets, which I did not continue after this year since the Norfolk
Opera Player's magazine, for which I wrote these verses, petered out.

Now we have reached September '75
With *Tales of Hoffman* waiting to be told.
Forward we go again to strain and strive
As avidly as some would dig for gold.
What is the secret of this mad compulsion,
The reason for the fervour, on a Monday?
Doubtless that singing is the main propulsion
(Sotto voce from Tuesday until Sunday?)
But this is more than just a Monday brightened
For comradeship is there, and fun is rife
So whilst the quality of sound is heightened
So also is the quality of life.
But we must bring this quality to bear
In presentations of the highest count.
No matter what we get in coming here,
It's really what we give that's paramount.
Unanimous we are in this resolve –
Diversified effecting its achievement.
While music, drama, dancing all involve,
Other allied activities are seething.

Scenery, costumes, properties and scores
Concerts and concert parties, social functions,
Administrative and financial chores,
Raffles and coffee, and other healing unctions.
Royalties, contracts, members to recruit,
Jumble sales and stalls in Earlham Park.
Make-up, with arts tonsorial or hirsute
And barbeques on beaches after dark.
Orchestral players, new and proven faces,
Tickets and programmes, front of house contriving;
Lighting, stage management, rehearsal places,
Auditioning for parts – and still surviving!
Committee meetings, secretaries various,
Orchestral music, library, lighting cues;
Publicity with matters multifarious
And Press reports to stimulate or bruise.
Photographs and archives, tape recordings,
Banner painting, scenery transportation.
Early ticket sales, and bills on hoardings;
Insurances for every situation.
All these things, some small, some monumental
Festoon each operatic presentation
Coessentially coincidental
Till final night with mayor and corporation.
Instruction all the time is all pervading –
Producer, pianist, dancer or M.D.
Infusing by seduction or upbraiding
Music, drama and choreography.
So let us carry on this happy hobby
With everybody being somebody,
Which means of course that no one's anybody
Excepting that they all are N.O.P.

The programme extract below and the photographs will, I hope, qualify, to some extent, the content of my versifying.

The building of sets for Norfolk Opera Players productions had first been accomplished in the barn at Wensum Lodge, with occasional assistance from the two small children of Ken and Brenda Davies, who then managed the Wensum Lodge complex. Robin and Julia Newson performed miraculously in this activity in those earlier days, but by this time the talented Alan Temple had taken over, and we had moved the operation centre from the barn (due to developments there) to the old gymnasium at Britannia Barracks. Since these memoirs are about musical matters, I won't go further into the practical issues of presenting opera. However, it would be remiss of me not to mention a name, which is

CAST (in order of appearance)

LINDORF	Robert Arnett
ANDREAS	Ernest Shaves
LUTHER	Phillip Chapman
NATHANIEL	Vernon Holt
HERMANN	Colin Thackery
HOFFMANN	Brian Tuffrey
NICKLAUS	Janet Arnett
SPALANZANI	Christopher Speake
COCHENILLE	Roy Emerson
COPPELIUS	Robert Arnett
OLYMPIA	Maria Daly
ANTONIA	Sally Stock
CRESPEL	Trevor Thurston
FRANZ	Christopher Speake
DR. MIRACLE	Robert Worley
THE VOICE	Kathleen Chapman
GIULIETTA	Ann Youngman
SCHLEMIL	Trevor Thurston
PITICHINACCIO	Vernon Holt
DAPERTUTTO	Robert Yates

Waiters, Students, Guests, Masqueraders and Servants:
Sylvia Bailey, Felicity Carr, Greta Carver, Kathleen Chapman, Gail Cullington, Hannelore Edwards, Myra Francis, Dilys Green, Christine Hawes, Noreen Hawes, Yvonne Ireson, Pamela Ivett, Christine Jenner, Pat Leggett, Pamela Marshall, Anne Piper, Sue Prutton, Anne Sayer, Vi Shaves, Phyllis Smith, Barbara Shorten, Liz Symons, Pat Tegerdine, Joan Thackery, Jill Thompson, Muriel Thompson, Joan Uff, Gwen Walker, Rosalind Wilkinson, Audrey Yates.

Bill Bailey, Ernest Becket, Phillip Chapman, Crispin Clark, Harry Dawson, Paul England, Roy Emerson, Richard Green, Maurice Grief, Alan Griffiths, Colin Harris, Des Holmes, Vernon Holt, Ken Howes, Ron Lyons, Tony Morris, Don Prutton, Larry Randall, Ernest Shaves, Derek Smithson, Colin Thackery, Robert Worley, Tom Wilkinson, Keith Wincote.

Dancers: Christine Hawes, Anne Piper, Joan Thackery, Rosalind Wilkinson, Colin Harris, Ernest Shaves, Colin Thackery, Keith Wincote.

Stewart Wrightson (East Anglia) Ltd., Incorporated Insurance Brokers, sponsored this page, and we record our grateful thanks

ORCHESTRA

First Violins	Peter Smith (Leader), Leslie Hallett, David Reeve, Stephen Bentley, Adrian Bassett
Second Violins	Rosalind Wills, Heather Bradshaw, Geoffrey Foot, Thelma Cook
Violas	George Milnes, Charles Parsons, Carol Jones
Cellos	Barry Wright, Francis Kapherr, Carol Pinching, Valerie Crome
Bass	Reginald Cadywould, Richard Stanley
Flutes	Nicholas Andrews, Angela Warne
Oboes	John Rose, Richard Danby
Clarinets	Roger Miller, Penelope Brown
Bassoons	Glyn Thomas, Isabel Ansell
Horns	J. Whatsize, Lynn Roberts, Susan Moulder
Trumpets	David Brook, Pamela Thaxton
Trombones	Dennis Wick, Jonathan Wilby, Ian Murray
Percussion	Angus Honeyman, Andrew Ansell, Nicholas Marshall

ACKNOWLEDGEMENTS

Scenery—Designed by Alan Temple and constructed by members and friends of the Society under the supervision of Brian Dack.
Costumes—Ladies' costumes made by ladies of the Society under the direction of the Wardrobe Mistresses Hadie Griffiths, Noreen Hawes and Gwynne Hooks.
Men's costumes and wigs by Wm. Mutrie & Son. Ltd., Edinburgh.
Electricians—David Hipperson, Robert Forster, Prue Willday.
Stage Managers—Alan Temple, Robert Hawes.
Properties—Jenny Crowley, Sandy Phillips, Margaret Goodchild.
Make-up—Janet Grimes and team.
Lighting Cues—Wendy Pepperell
Back Stage Manager—Leslie Malyon.
Front of House Manager—Wilfred Rush.
Call 'Boy'—April Ireson.
Rehearsal Pianists—John King, Judy Tovey.
Librarian—Harry Dawson.
Publicity Secretary—Ernest Becket.
Painting of Banners—Malcolm Ireson.
Our grateful thanks are extended to friends who are acting as programme sellers and to all other individuals and organisations who have assisted in this presentation.

We record our appreciation to Bush Builders (Norwich) Ltd., who have kindly sponsored this page

Tales of Hoffman – Norfolk Opera Players at St Andrew's Hall

shown in the programme as the painter of banners. Malcolm Ireson did a great deal more than this. He transported scenery from the barracks and later still from obscure map references, and joined Robert F Foster and the other electricians in scaling the heights of St Andrew's Hall to install a battery of spotlights. Tribute must also be paid to Colin Thackery who devoted such resourcefulness and energy to the task of master-minding the storage and disposition of scenery in its many and varied requirements. There were, of course, many others too numerous to mention here, who gave of their energy and expertise, but who will recognise themselves from my versifying in Chapter 29.

St Andrew's Hall has no orchestra pit, so in presenting *Tales of Hoffman* I decided that the orchestra should be sited at the side of the hall (stage left), suitably cloaked from the audience. With the assistance of closed circuit television, provided by University of East Anglia (courtesy of John Grey) we the singers were able to see the conductor through three television monitors placed above stage, left, right and centre. It worked well.

I booked a week in January for future years. January is a difficult month because of weather conditions and various viruses, which seem to be surging around, affecting singers and potential audiences alike. However it was the only week available for an on-going booking. A January performance did have an advantage, in that Dick Condon would be presenting pantomime at the Theatre until early February, so that we couldn't be sandwiched between Glyndebourne opera and Sadlers Wells ballet, as was once the case.

Harking back to *Tales of Hoffman* for a moment, there are two small incidents that I remember vividly. The first concerns Lesli Kurl of whom I have spoken earlier. At the end of the Saturday performance, two figures could be seen walking from the rear of the hall, towards the stage. 'My God,' I said to myself, 'it's Leslie' (I never *thought* 'Lesli') It was. He had a friend with him. He gave a short oration, which milked the audience of further applause. This was vintage 'Leslie'.

The other incident relates to a performance earlier in the week. I was angry with someone, or everyone – I can't remember why, but, ignoring the normal procedure of removing greasepaint etc before going home, I decided to depart immediately, prevailing upon Audrey and another of the cast (a car passenger) to do likewise. For this opera there was no contralto role for Audrey, and Richard White, producer, had given Audrey the role of a waiter, complete with moustache (vintage Richard).

It so happened that this was the first day on which a one-way system had been operating in St Benedict's Street, but my thoughts were undoubtedly homicidal, so I decided to go straight through (the wrong way). A Panda car was stationed at the bottom of Grapes Hill. The lady police driver summoned me to stop. It must have been a stern test for both her and me, but she must have been told to be lenient on the first day of one-way traffic, because we continued our journey home, I in full, fierce make-up, my front-seat passenger arrayed as a Venetian courtesan, and Audrey in the back wearing a moustache.

The Tales of Hoffman. **Left to right: Robert Yates, Ann Youngman, Brian Tuffrey and Colin Thackery**

Rita Green and I sang in a Brahm's *Requiem* at Fakenham. I have always enjoyed immensely the baritone solos in this work. John Winsworth led the orchestra and Bill Purchase conducted the choir and orchestra.

Audrey and I performed in yet another *Messiah* at Cromer. This time it was *Messiah* from Scratch, a sort of presentation which was becoming increasingly popular at that time, 'a performance without rehearsal for choirs and individuals and listeners'. Sally Stock, soprano, and Brian Tuffrey, tenor, also the Sheringham & Cromer Choral Society performed. All visiting singers were conducted by Howard Rooke, and Donald Spinks was the organist.

Rita Green, David Clark and I sang in Haydn's *Creation* as part of a Dereham Festival. The Mid-Norfolk Singers augmented by 'Singers and Orchestra from Dereham and district' performed under the baton of David Kett.

Selections from *Messiah* at St Mary's Baptist Church was unusual, in that performances there as I have previously noted were normally a reciprocal arrangement with Sheringham and Cromer Choral Society. On this occasion it was St Mary's Choir only, with Cyril Pearce as organist. Kathleen Chapman was the soprano soloist, and Keith Wincote, the tenor. No mention is made in the programme of a conductor, so I imagine it must have been Cyril Pearce.

Now we come to *Noye's Fludde* at St John's Catholic Cathedral, in which Audrey and I sang Mrs Noye (Noah) and Mr Noye respectively. The remaining cast were girls of the Notre Dame School.

We rehearsed at the School, and performed in the Catholic Cathedral on three days in June. I have mentioned the acoustics of this establishment before. Our earlier experiences forewarned us, but did nothing to overcome the problems of performing under the central tower. Audrey and I had difficulties enough. The young girls had even more, with voices not having reached maturity. It was a great shame, because they all did so well. We can only hope that voices were more audible to the audience than they were from one performer to another. Vyvyan Morris who was head of music at the Notre Dame, was an excellent musical director.

Antony Hopkins was again presenting one of his works at the 1976 Triennal Festival. This time it was *Rich Man, Poor Man*, an opera for children with one or two adult soloists. A professional tenor, Bernard Dickerson, took the main part. I have no programme of the event, and I can only assume from a perusal of the rehearsal notes that I must have taken the part of the Bishop. I can't really remember much about it, except that it was staged at the Theatre Royal, and that it furthered my acquaintance with Antony Hopkins. We trudged through Norwich together between morning and afternoon rehearsals on Sunday 10th October in search of a 'tea and wad'.

Frederick (Fred) Firth was prominent in the rehearsals, as he had been with *In The Beginning* in 1970. Fred was then Music Advisor for the Norwich City Council, later to become Music Adviser for the City and County.

We enjoyed a good relationship with Fred, who was involved at the highest level with music in Norwich. He was an outstanding boy soprano, contemporaneous with the Temple chorister Ernest Lough who in the nineteen twenties had met with so much acclaim. Fred had made a 78 rpm record of a selection of songs and arias in the North of England at that time. As I write, a compact disc has recently been made of prominent boy soprano soloists of the pre-war era. The solos on Fred's 78 record are on the disc, and the beauty of tone and musicianship displayed are impressive.

Gordon Hawkins once again prevailed upon me to sing in a performance of Haydn's *Creation* (Part I only) at Tacket Street United Reformed Church, Ipswich. The soprano and tenor were either professionals or local singers.

We staged a 'Come into the Parlour' at the Assembly House, with Charles Roberts compèring. The concert was presented by the Thorpe St Andrew Rotary Club in aid of the furnishing and equipping of the new Norfolk Hostel for the Deaf. Perhaps I might be permitted to quote from the Press critique on this occasion? 'with the decorously dapper Mr Charles Roberts as Master of Ceremonies. His eulogistic eloquence was exemplary in introducing four veritable vocalists from our lusty locale – the colourful coloratura of Mrs Rita Green, the mellow maturity of Mrs Audrey Yates, the sublime sonority of her husband, Mr Robert Yates, and the vibrant vivacity of our clerical chanteur of Colegate, the Rev David Clark'. David Forshaw was our impeccable pianist.

Another performance of *Messiah* concluded our performances of serious music in this year. This took place at St Andrew's School, Thorpe St Andrew, with the 'Combined choir – pupils and friends – concert orchestra', with continuo by Dudley Bradshaw, whose daughter Lynda sang the soprano solos. Richard White was the tenor, and Geoffrey Pinching conducted. The Combined Schools Wind Band played *Christmas Festival* by Leroy Anderson.

Maddermarket Music Hall, as ever, concluded our year.

Chapter 30 - 1977

Cavalleria Rusticana and *I Pagliacci* (St Andrew's Hall, Norwich) ~
Messiah Beccles Church) ~ *Elijah* (Fakenham Church) ~ *Messiah*
(Cromer Church) ~ Come Into the Parlour (Assembly House, Norwich) ~
Recital (Aylsham Methodist Church) ~ Songs of Yesterday
(Thorpe Grammar School) ~ Recital (Church of St Andrew and St Peter,
Blofield) ~ *Merrie England* (concert version) (St Mary's Church,
Woodbridge) ~ Recital (Itteringham Festival, Itteringham Church) ~
Recital (Church of St Andrew and St Peter, Blofield) ~ Concert
(Methodist Schoolroom, Hethersett) ~ Messiah (Garland Street Baptist
Church, Bury St Edmunds) ~ Come Into the Parlour
(Brooke Village Hall) ~ Maddermarket Music Hall

This is the second year in which we presented opera at St Andrew's Hall. With
all its disadvantages, lack of proscenium arch, pillars impeding view, no orchestra
pit and, in some areas, difficult acoustical properties, it is an important building,
and one has a feeling of importance in being privileged to sing in it. Moreover,
we had imprinted our own personality upon its hallowed walls with a successful
performance of *Tales of Hoffman* last year. One great advantage in performing
there was that we used the adjoining Blackfriar's Hall as band room and dressing
rooms.

Cavalleria Rusticana (Mascagni) and *Pagliacci* (Leoncavallo) (known in the
trade as 'Cav and Pag') are traditionally linked in performance, and we saw no
reason to break the pattern. John Barnett was Musical Director for 'Cav' with
Maggie Teggin producing the opera, while Richard White produced 'Pag' with
Colin Goodchild as Musical Director. Dance arrangements were by Margot
Warne. The programme shows that we had forty-three ladies and twenty-three
men in the choruses. I have a cassette of 'Pag', and am rather proud of my
singing of the Prologue. Whether rightly so is for others to judge.

A word about the orchestra. Throughout my period as Administrator/
Chairman of the company, I consider myself extremely fortunate in being able,
with the collaboration of the Musical Director for the particular opera, to call
upon such talented musicians to accompany us so splendidly in our
performances with only three rehearsals – one on their own, the second a 'band
call' (soloists and sometimes chorus attending) and then the dress rehearsal.

To save my reeling off a list of names, I reproduce two pages of the
programme for these two works.(See following page)

In an effort to avoid being tedious, allow me to chronicle the following
events, all performed before and including April 7th.

Messiah at Beccles with Valerie Walker, Audrey Mitchell and John Roper,
and Reginald Firth conducting an orchestra led by Richard Featherstone.

An *Elijah* at Fakenham with Rita Green, Elizabeth Gould and Brian Tuffrey,
and Bill Purchase conducting an orchestra led by Norman Moor.

ORCHESTRA

Violins	Paul Clarke (Leader), Adrian Bassett, Ken Boast, Jill Brett, Joan Brewer, Eric Burdett, Thelma Cooke, Nora Pearson, Jennifer Pinching, David Reeve, Sally Tudge.
Violas	Sylvia Ord, Jean Langdale-Pope, Wendy Ward.
Cellos	Barry Wright, Carol Pinching, Francis Kapherr, Clare Spelman.
Bass	Christopher Williams, Timothy Collins.
Flutes	Michael Butcher, Bridget Rogers.
Clarinet	Marion Danby, Penelope Brown.
Oboe/Cor Anglais	John Rose.
Bassoons	Isobell Ansel, Glynn Thomas.
Horns	James Whatsize, Peter Wheales.
Trumpets	David Woodrow, John Landymore.
Trombone	Derrick Wick.
Percussion	Angus Honeyman, Colin Brady.
Harp	Martin Wyatt.

ACKNOWLEDGEMENTS

Scenery—Constructed by members and friends of the Society under the supervision of John Ward. Principals' costumes Pagliacci and complete wardrobe for Cavalleria Rusticana from Wm. Mutrie & Son Ltd., Edinburgh.

Remainder of the costumes made by members of the Society and friends under the direction of the Wardrobe Mistresses: Helen Griffiths, Noreen Hawes and Gwynne Hooks.

Electricians—David Hipperson, Robert Forster, Peter Thackery.
Stage Manager—Gordon Marshall.
Properties—Bob Worley.
Make-up—Janet Grimes and team.
Lighting Cues—Judy Tovey, Wendy Pepperell.
Front of House Manager—Wilfred Rush.
Call 'Boy'—Jenny Reid.
Rehearsal Pianists—John King, Judy Tovey.
Librarian—Harry Dawson.
Publicity Secretary—Ernest Becket.
Painting of Banners—Malcolm Ireson.

Our grateful thanks are extended to friends who are acting as programme sellers and to all other individuals and organisations who have assisted in this presentation.

NORFOLK OPERA PLAYERS

Committee: Robert Yates (Chairman/Administrator), Alan Griffiths (Treasurer), Barbara Shorten (Secretary), Ernest Becket, Roy Emerson, Gwynne Hooks, Yvonne Ireson, Derek Smithson, Colin Thackery, Richard White, Ann Youngman.

Social Committee: Bill Bailey, Sylvia Bailey, Pat Tegerdine, Joan Thackery, Muriel Thompson.

CAST in order of appearance:

CAVALLERIA RUSTICANA

Santuzza, a village girl	Sally Stock
Mamma Lucia, Turiddu's mother	Greta Carver
Alfio, the village carter	Robert Arnett
Turiddu, a young villager	Brian Tuffrey
Lola, Alfio's wife	Kathleen Chapman

PAGLIACCI

Tonio (Taddeo) a clown	Robert Yates
Peppe (Harlequin)	Keith Wincote
Nedda (Columbine) Canio's wife	Ann Youngman
Canio (Pagliaccio) leader of a troupe of strolling players	Vernon Holt
Silvio, a villager	Maurice Bird
Two villagers	Colin Thackery
	Leslie Malyon

Ladies of the Chorus

Janet Arnett, Sylvia Bailey, Freda Broady, Sheila Box, Felicity Carr, Kathleen Chapman, Sylvia Constance, Heidi Cracknell, Carol Deane-White, Hannelore Edwards, Dilys Green, Christine Hawes, Noreen Hawes, Kay Holmes, April Ireson, Yvonne Ireson, Pam Ivett, Christina Jenner, Karen Joyce, Linda Knights, Pat Leggett, Gladys Malyon, Pam Marshall, Ann Piper, Sue Prutton, Judy Reid, Vi Shaves, Barbara Shorten, Jill Shorten, Phyllis Smith, Hilary Smythe, Sybil Snelling, Norma Speake, Liz Symonds, Pat Tegerdine, Joan Thackery, Jill Thompson, Muriel Thompson, Susan Tuck, Joan Ulf, Bobbie White, Ros Wilkinson, Audrey Yates.

Gentlemen of the Chorus

Bill Bailey, Ernest Becket, Philip Chapman, Crispin Clark, Harry Dawson, Paul England, Dick Green, Maurice Grief, Alan Griffiths, Ken Howes, Leslie Malyon, Don Morris, Don Prutton, Larry Randall, Ernie Shaves, Mervyn Shore, Derek Smithson, Chris Speake, Colin Thackery, Trevor Thurston, Tom Wilkinson, Alan Willoughby, George Wright.

Children

Jill Bailey, Angela Moore, Jill Shorten, Tim Howes, Andrew Shorten

Dancers

April Ireson, Lindsey Ray

This page has been sponsored by Margaret's Florists, Reepham Road and Timberhill and Andrea Fashions of London Street, Norwich, to whom we are very grateful

Dixons D.I.Y. Store, Reepham Road, Norwich, sponsored this page and we record our grateful thanks

'Cav' and 'Pag' at St Andrew's Hall, Norwich

A *Messiah* from Scratch at Cromer with Lesley Brownhill, Elizabeth Gould and David Clark, conducted by Howard Rooke and accompanied on the organ by Michael Allard.

'Gratified by the approval bestowed upon the artistes at a previous evening of melodious entertainment of a most decorous character, the organisers make bold to present a further soirée of seemly song. With, we trust, not unbecoming modesty, they offer delectation and delight – a further programme of Victorian and Edwardian ballads to benefit that most estimable of causes – The Silver Jubilee Appeal of Her Most Gracious Majesty Queen Elizabeth II' – (Admission by programme – One Sovereign). This is how the front cover of our second 'Come Into the Parlour' concert at the Assembly House read. I can't remember who composed those words, but I suspect Charles Roberts, who again compèred. Thorpe St Andrew's Rotary Club were again presenting, and I believe that the Silver Jubilee Appeal was well rewarded, both artistically and financially. A Flower Festival at Aylsham Methodist Church included a display by Audrey of suede garments, hand-stitched and thonged leatherwork, rush work and table lamps. These were products of a more or less commercial venture, which Audrey had set up after ceasing her work as Crafts Organiser for the Disabled Association, during which voluntary employment she had learnt and taught many crafts. The enterprise was entitled 'Norfolk Thong Things' and had musical connotations in that Audrey was forever singing 'with a thong in my heart'. She shared this enterprise with Ros Wilkinson who, on this occasion offered items of jewellery.

But I digress from the purpose of mentioning the Flower Festival in these memoirs, which is that we sang in the church, together with Kathleen Chapman and Brian Tuffrey with Judy Tovey as accompanist. Judy of course was a well-known pianist, one with whom we had already worked, and would be more involved later on.

Charles Roberts recruited us again to present 'Songs of Yesterday' at Thorpe Grammar School – 'an evening of music and the spoken word in the spirit of Victorian and Edwardian days. (Admission 50p – Children and Pensioners 25p – pay at the door). Rita Green sang with us, but not David Clark. Richard Forshaw was again the accompanist, Coral Newell joined Charles in readings, and the Barbershop Singers contributed, conducted by Mrs Rosemary Kimmins. We took Kathleen Chapman, Janet Arnett and Vernon Holt with us to sing in a concert version of *Merrie England* for the Woodbridge Choral Society. This was another undertaking of our old friend Gordon Hawkins, who conducted. The occasion was memorable (apart from the concert itself which I think went well) for the fact that in driving home in our Dormobile (with the entire cast) I found myself driving the wrong way on a dual carriageway. You have to have some luck in life, don't you?

Another Festival, this time at Itteringham, included an evening in the church with Audrey and myself, with Judy Tovey accompanying and also contributing piano solos. Also appearing was the Reverend Fred Pratt-Green who read poetry. The Reverend 'Fred' was well known for his hymn compositions.

Audrey, again accompanied by the excellent Judy Tovey, sang two groups of songs in a concert at Blofield Church in May, presented by Blofield Music and Arts Guild. Also included were 'Two Elegiac Poems' by Lesli Kurl (remember him?) written for flute, oboe and piano, and realised by Bridget Rogers, Alison Clouting and Judith Constable respectively.

In September I contributed two groups of songs to another Blofield concert, with Elizabeth Rooke my accompanist, and with Roger Rayner providing piano solos.

A concert at Hethersett included Tony and Heidi Blythe (now Heidi Yates – not related) Howard and Elizabeth Rooke (piano duets) and Mary Alger (flute).

Rita and Richard were again with us at Bury St Edmunds to sing another *Messiah*, with John Ince at the organ.

Then another evening at Brooke compèred by Charles Roberts – 'An Evening of Victorian and Edwardian Songs and Ballads of a nature received with acclaim in the most elegant soirees and calculated to enchant the most discerning of ears'. This was another Silver Jubilee concert, as were most of the others in this year, this one presented by The Friends of the Norwich Museums.

Forgive me for mentioning that we concluded the year with Maddermarket Music Hall.

By courtesy of Eastern Counties Newspapers
After 'Come into the Parlour' at the Assembly House. Left to right: Robert Yates, Richard Forshaw, Charles Roberts, the Revd David Clark Rita Green, Audrey Yates

Chapter 31 - 1978

**Nabucco (St Andrew's Hall, Norwich) ~ Words & Music (Costessey
Methodist Church) ~ Mozart's *Coronation Mass* and Fauré's *Requiem*
(Fakenham Parish Church) ~ *Elijah* (St Mary's Church, Southtown,
Great Yarmouth) ~ Vaughan Williams' *Sea Symphony* (Cromer Church)
~ *Dido and Aeneas* (concert version) (Gresham's School, Holt) ~ *Messiah*
(Fakenham Church) ~ Maddermarket Music Hall**

I think that *Nabucco* at St Andrew's Hall really suited the ambience of that
historic building. We had a chorus of sixty and a cast of eight soloists. The
opening chorus (truly Verdi) seemed to imperil the very structure of the
building. With the Society's acquisition of two other bass/baritone soloists, I now
was ceasing to audition for leading roles, and was quite content to join the
chorus of the opera, knowing that the roles of Zachariah and the High Priest of
Baal were in the excellent hands of Robert Worley and Robert Arnett. Other
roles were taken by Heidi Blithe, Brian Tuffrey, Sally Stock, Maurice Bird, Sybil
Snelling and Christopher Speake. Three children were also included - Jill Bailey,
Tim Howes and Angela Moore.

Audrey and I performed in 'Words and Music for Good Friday' at Costessey
Methodist Church, joining other soloists from the Church choir.

Mozart's *Coronation Mass* and Fauré's *Requiem* followed the evening service
at Fakenham Parish Church and we joined Alison Humphries, Richard White,
Darren Bridge (treble) and the Lowestoft Choral Society in a performance of
Elijah at St Mary's Church, Southtown, Great Yarmouth.

Vaughan Williams' *Sea Symphony* was the ambitious choice of Howard
Rooke, for performance by the Sheringham and Cromer Choral Society.
Soprano and baritone soloists are involved in this work, and the soprano listed in
the programme was Lesley Brownhill. She was unable to perform because of
illness, and Alison Humphries took her place. It is an exciting work and quite
demanding, but the choir met its demands, and (I think) so did the soloists. The
second half of this evening's concert was devoted to a performance of
Beethoven's *Choral Fantasia*, a work for pianoforte, orchestra and chorus. The
pianist for this work was Elizabeth Rooke, (Howard Rooke's wife), who you will
remember had accompanied me at the Blofield Church in 1977, playing
brilliantly on each of these two occasions.

Audrey sang the parts of Sorceress and Spirit in a performance of Purcell's
Dido and Aeneas at Gresham's school, with Rita Green as Dido, Carole Bower as
Belinda and Steve Benson as Aeneas.

A *Messiah* in Fakenham Church concluded the 'serious' musical activities of
the year, but yes, we finished as ever in a lighter vein at the Maddermarket.

Chapter 32 - 1979

I Lombardi (Norwich Cathedral) ~ Dvorak's *Stabat Mater* (Hingham Church) ~ Recital (Aylsham Town Hall) ~ Recital (Thurne Methodist Chapel) ~ Beethoven's *Mass In C* (Fakenham Church) ~ *The Beggar's Opera* (Sewell Barn Theatre, Norwich) ~ *Noye's Fludde* (The Lancastrian School, Fakenham) ~ Maddermarket Music Hall

We were to perform Verdi's *I Lombardi* at St Andrew's Hall in January, but a week before our scheduled date the manual staff went on strike in response to a national union resolution. I went to speak to them, but there was nothing they could do. At an urgently convened meeting, I asked all members to search around for an alternative venue. I declared that the show must go on, even if we had to perform it in the underpass at the top of St Stephens.

As it happened we were very fortunate. Michael Nicholas, who was at that time a member of the City Council, telephoned me to say that he had heard, in committee, of our dilemma, and would we like to present our opera at the Cathedral? We would, and we did. Maggie Teggin was producing this opera, and I convened a meeting of the entire company at the Cathedral, at which we discussed how the transfer could be accomplished.

Maggie was excellent in supervising the necessary alterations to the staging and wrote copious notes to all performers which were placed strategically in dressing rooms, and points of stage entries – all this before dress rehearsal. We had to build a stage, and install an additional electricity supply to the Cathedral, to support our lighting requirements. This necessitated breaking a clerestory window to bring in the cable. It was a massive operation for Robert Forster, who had already distinguished himself in our St Andrew's Hall presentations, the lighting of which required steeplejack nerves, as well as technical expertise. Joining him in these enterprises were the ever-willing and competent Malcolm Ireson and Bill Bailey.

The weather was cold, and the country was snow-bound. Whilst the male cast were to use the North Transept as a changing room (discreetly screened), the ladies of the cast had been accorded dressing room facilities at Norwich School. The approach to the Cathedral from the school necessitated crossing the ice-bound playground. One of the scenes in *I Lombardi* featured ladies of the harem. (I wonder if Michael Nicholas knew this when he invited us!) Imagine therefore the ladies in their flimsy nighties crossing the ice-bound playground, in dim lighting. It is not surprising therefore that one of them suffered a fall and resultant arm fracture.

The wintry conditions did not prevent the North Yorkshire Operatic Society bringing a party of its members from Leeds. They were interested because they were to present *I Lombardi* themselves in the near future.

The change of venue was a bit too much for Maurice Grief. He was ageing, and found difficulty in re-orientating himself in the new surroundings. He was now becoming a bit of a responsibility on stage (in our performance of *Faust* at the Theatre Royal for instance, a pair of trousers were distinctly visible under his monk's garb). This had prompted Maggie Teggin to commission me to take him off after my short solo. I explained this to Maurice, but at the first night's performance, he showed a reluctance to leave the chorus, and it was with some difficulty that I managed to impel his twenty stone frame towards the wings. I remonstrated with him, and he appeared contrite, but the following night he refused to come and I had to leave him, because a bout of wrestling would seem out of context with what was being enacted. Further remonstration provoked Maurice to say: 'Well, I like singing that chorus.' The third night he not only refused to come, but tried to stop me from making my exit. I read the riot act to him after the performance, and declared that if he did not comply with the producer's instructions, he would be out of the show. On the following evening, I was pressed hard against one of the flats, to enable the chorus of Crusaders to pass by. Maurice was amongst them. He paused, legs astride, arms akimbo, he and I eyeball to eyeball, and in his resonant Norfolk accent, said: 'Bob – d'ye still love me?'

I have already extolled the virtues of those steadfast and capable members who construct, paint and transport scenery. All of these were in action at the Cathedral. The set design was by the wonderful Anna Welbourne and scenery construction under the supervision of Colin Thackery was adapted to the requirements of the new venue.

So far, in this narrative I have not made mention of the storage of scenery. Having been stored earlier at Wensum Lodge barn, (before its conversion to teaching rooms) and at Brittania Barracks old gymnasium, it now reposed, between operas, at a barn 'out in the sticks' owned by farmer John Green, to whom Norfolk Opera Players have been indebted ever since (at least, up to the time of my writing these memoirs). Here again, I pay tribute to Malcolm Ireson for arranging transport to and fro.

In spite of all its problems, *I Lombardi* went well. Frederick Firth did a splendid job as musical director. I have not listed everyone involved, but the following programme extract will, I hope, supplement information I have given.

CAST
in order of appearance

PAGANO, Son of Folco	*ROBERT WORLEY †MAURICE BIRD
ARVINO, Son of Folco	VERNON HOLT
GISELDA, Daughter of Arvino and Viclinda	*SALLY STOCK †ANN YOUNGMAN
VICLINDA, Wife of Arvino	... JUDY REID
PIRRO, Equerry of Pagano	TREVOR THURSTON
PRIOR	ALAN WILLOUGHBY
ACCIANO, Tyrant of Antioch	ROBERT YATES
ORONTE, Son of Acciano and Sofia	BRIAN TUFFREY
SOFIA, Wife of Acciano	SYBIL SNELLING

* Monday, Wednesday, Friday
† Tuesday, Thursday, Saturday

Dennis Johnson asked Audrey and me to contribute to a performance by Norwich Singers of Dvorak's *Stabat Mater* at Hingham Church, with Rita Green and Brian Tuffrey as the other two soloists and Bernard Burrell as organist.

We performed at Aylsham again. I think it must have been either at the Methodist Church or the Town Hall. The Aylsham Brass Band was prominent and Audrey and I, together with Leslie Mallyon and Sybil Snelling, sang songs, duets and quartets.

At Thurne Methodist Church Kathleen Chapman, Leslie Mallyon and Phillip Chapman joined us in presenting a concert for our old friend Clifford Cooke.

Bill Purchase, conductor of the Fakenham Musical Society, invited Audrey and me, together with Alison Humphreys and Brian Tuffrey to sing in Beethoven's *Mass in C*. Also on the programme was Benjamin Britten's *St Nicholas*. Kenneth Woollam, principal tenor of English National Opera was engaged to sing the role of Saint Nicholas.

By courtesy of Eastern Counties Newspapers

The Beggar's Opera, Norfolk Opera Players' first performance at the Sewell Barn.

Mr Peachum (Robert Yates) with Polly Peachum (Sybil Snelling) and Lucy Locket (Heidi Blyth)

In the administration of Norfolk Opera Players, I had always sought to employ its members according to their ability. Some were excellent chorus members and were content to serve in that capacity. Others aspired to leading roles, and it was with this in mind, and also the need to present some profitable operas, that, during my years with the company, I endeavoured to present two operas each year, one large, one small. Ever questing for the means to use as much as possible of our Norfolk Opera Players' solo talent, whether established or otherwise, I was very happy to be advised by Roy Emerson that we could possibly present small operas at the Sewell Barn Theatre if I spoke to Valerie Glauert, then Headmistress of the Blyth/Jex school. The property belonged to the school, and was once the barn in which Anna Sewell (author of *Black Beauty*) stabled the horse, which inspired the book. Her brother owned the house, which is now part of the school. The barn had recently been converted into a small theatre seating 100 people, with tiered seats rising up steeply on three sides of the acting area.

A successful chat with Valerie Glauert led to our using the theatre for the first public presentation in November. We chose John Gay's *The Beggar's Opera*.

In the seven previous performances of this opera in which Audrey and I had appeared, I had played Captain Macheath and Audrey had played Mrs Peachum. The fate of contraltos is such that in opera they are usually cast as elderly ladies. Consequently Audrey, when quite young, had played Mrs Peachum, judiciously made up. Now she was again cast in the role. I conceded Macheath to a younger man and settled for Mr Peachum, a part that I enjoyed.

Bridget Grief, one of the founder members of Norfolk Opera Players had gained some experience in producing and was asked to produce this ballad opera, with Norma Wick as her assistant. This was a new venture for Norma. She did very well, and has produced several musical works since then.

Later that month, Audrey and I were invited to take the parts of Mr and Mrs Noye (Noah) in *Noye's Fludde* by Benjamin Britten, at the Lancastrian School (High School) at Fakenham. Fifty students sang and acted, and members of the school orchestra joined the instrumentalists to play under the baton of Bill Purchase. We find this an attractive work, and enjoyed the Fakenham presentation. In all the musical works involving children with which we have been concerned, we have always been very impressed with the dedication of those participating, and the considerable charm of their performances. Fakenham was no exception.

Maddermarket Music Hall to finish the year once again. In one of our acts, we used a song entitled 'Love, Could I Only Tell Thee'. The action was a little less subtle than our other contributions. I wore a pair of trousers made for someone twice my girth. I sang with hands in pockets, until Audrey handed me the aspidistra. I had to take it. Need I say more? I hasten to add that I was discreetly clad underneath.

Chapter 33 - 1980

Prince Igor (St Andrew's Hall, Norwich) ~ Fauré's *Requiem* and Bach's
Magnificat (St Peter's Church, Sheringham) ~ Francis Westbrook's
Calvary (Christ Church, Ipswich) ~ *The Crucifixion* (Fakenham Church)
~ *Elijah* (Starston Church) ~ *Christmas Oratorio* (Fakenham Church) ~
The Marriage (Sewell Barn Theatre, Norwich) ~ *Festival of Carols*
(St Peter Mancroft Church, Norwich) ~ Brahms' *Requiem* (Town Hall,
Great Yarmouth) ~ Maddermarket Music Hall.

We were now established at St Andrew's Hall, presenting opera in its once
hallowed, and now, at least, prestigious ambience, with all the difficulties of
staging, and its variable acoustical properties. Nevertheless, in January, with the
Theatre Royal Pantomime still playing, we were safe from being sandwiched
between professional opera or ballet companies.

I invited Mike Anderson of Anglia Television to produce *Prince Igor*. Early
rehearsals persuaded him that the story was insufficient for him to work on, and
he withdrew.

Our old friend Professor Humphrey Proctor-Gregg again provided us with
his English translation, but we were obliged to obtain vocal scores from
Germany. The alternative would have been to buy them at a cost of £25 each
score. Happily one of our members, Hannelore Edwards, spoke fluent German,
which facilitated the undertaking. I think we must have hired the orchestral
scores from one of the English publishers, but my old files are not in my
possession, so I cannot give details.

Upon Mike Anderson's withdrawal, we invited Peter Spalding to produce
the opera. Like most of those who, over the years, were invited to produce or
musically direct our productions, this was his first venture into grand opera,
although he had been involved with us in a Gilbert and Sullivan opera, and he
was teacher of drama at Keswick Hall (then a Teacher Training College).

He chose to dispense with our scenery flats, and relied on the natural
atmosphere and construction of the building to provide a background to the
story. Colin Goodchild, now a veteran of Norfolk Opera Players presentations,
was appointed musical director.

The opera includes the famous Palovtsian dances, and Margot Warne, with
her talented ladies of the Norwich Ballet Club, together with the superlative
athleticism of five members of the Priory Gym, brought great excitement to the
presentation, making it one of the highlights of the opera.

My own role in the opera was to play Prince Galitsky, brother of Prince
Igor's wife, the Princess Jaroslavna. Galitsky is altogether a nasty character –
could I have been type-cast? Prince Igor, conversely, is a 'goodie', despite doing
some rather ill-advised things. The music score gives him a beautiful aria, which
I have sung subsequently in the Russian language, which so much conveys the
drama of the piece. Explanation of my delving into the Russian language comes
later.

I reproduce an article by Jonathan Mardle, (Eric Fowler) who interviewed me around this time. It had the headline 'HIGH AMBITIONS'.

LESS than 15 years ago, in the optimism generated by what we called the affluent society, enthusiasts for the arts in Norwich were discussing an opera house, a big new concert hall, and a smaller theatre which was to accommodate a permanent professional repertory company. People quarrelled over these castles in the air. Nothing would do for the advocates of opera and ballet but a theatre built specifically for these purposes. They scorned the idea of improvising in the concert hall. Similarly, no existing theatre would do for the enthusiasts for drama.

Somehow, it seemed to be thought that by a combination of State, municipal and university patronage all these ambitions might be achieved. I look back to the 1950s and 1960s, in spite of all our fears and failings, as years of generous enthusiasm in this country. They were the years of raising the school leaving age, building new schools, founding new universities, constructing new towns — and, in the arts, establishing new festivals. The Prime Minister, then Mr. Harold Wilson, and after him Mr. Heath, were promising — fallaciously — to drag Britain kicking and screaming into a technological revolution. And, on the basis of the new wealth and leisure arising from applied science, the former nation of shopkeepers was also to become a nation of artists.

However, the vaulting ambitions of Norwich for opera house, concert hall and professional repertory theatre came down in the end to the municipal purchase and reconstruction of the Theatre Royal of the 1930s. It is far from the dreams of the 1960s, but as a civic theatre it contrives with remarkable success to be all things to all men, accommodating anything from Glyndbourne opera to Christmas pantomime, the Royal Shakespeare Company to bawdy modern farce, symphony orchestras to pop groups.

This is the old Norfolk and Norwich business of make do and mend. I sometimes wondered, in the optimism of the 1960s, whether we were about to become so highly equipped and professionalised in matters of the arts, that the local amateurs, upon whom we used to depend so heavily, would be eclipsed. In music, apart from the rare treat of the Triennial Festival, local orchestras and choral societies — performing as much for their own pleasure as that of the audience — formerly provided our staple fare from year to year. In drama, no. 2 touring companies came to the old Theatre Royal: but Nugent Monck, despairing of getting Shakespeare and the classics produced as he wanted them, in the commercial theatres of his day, came here to found, on a shoestring, the Norwich Players, and to exercise his art in the little Maddermarket Theatre with amateur actors. It seemed to me that, whatever privations we suffered in this backwater of England because of our remoteness from the main stream, we gained something from having to develop our own talents.

Well, in spite of the economic gloom that descended upon us in the 1970s, and deepens in 1980, there have been great and beneficial changes. The Aldeburgh and King's Lynn Festivals, the alliance of University, Philharmonic Society and Cathedral in Norwich music, and the visits of national opera, ballet and drama companies to the Theatre Royal, have opened fresh opportunities of hearing and seeing the best of music and drama. And the effect, so far from squashing the local amateurs, has been to stimulate them.

Which train of thought was prompted by a meeting last week with Mr. Robert Yates, who is both chairman and a leading singer of the Norfolk Opera Players. He told me how, some 20 years ago, he and a group of his friends got rather tired both of oratorio and of the alternation of Gilbert and Sullivan and elderly musical comedies which was the common repertoire of amateur operatic societies. They were challenged to form their own opera group, with ambitions to progress from comic to grand opera. They started with "The Beggar's Opera" at the Maddermarket. Then, reverting to Gilbert and Sullivan, they produced "Patience" at Cromer Pier Pavilion, and came away with a profit of £1 2s. 7½d.

Performing where they could, and gradually accumulating new singers and players, financial support and stage equipment, they went on, down the years, from Offenbach to Donizetti, to Smetana's "Bartered Bride" and Gounod's "Faust," until they arrived, in 1978 and 1979, at no less a composer than Verdi. His "I Lombardi," in Norwich Cathedral last January, was their boldest effort. But certainly not less temerarious is their current production in St. Andrew's Hall of Borodin's "Prince Igor" an opera which is pervaded by memories of the great Chaliapin, and which is moreover such an elaborate and spectacular combination of opera and ballet that it is not often performed.

I found myself, at Mr. Yates' invitation, at a dress rehearsal on Sunday evening, with Norfolk enthusiasts variously attired as medieval Russian soldiers and peasants and Tartar warriors. Even in a truncated version of the opera, and in a stage setting which is inevitably an improvisation, the spirited music makes its effect, and the performers' enjoyment is infectious. I doubt whether we shall ever arrive at the artistic millennium discussed in the 1960s, of our own opera house, a new concert hall and a professional repertory theatre. The economic climate in 1980 is not propitious but meanwhile, the local amateurs certainly do not lack courage or ambition in making music for themselves.

I performed in Fauré's *Requiem* and Bach's *Magnificat* with the Sheringham and Cromer Choral Society, with an orchestra led by Frederic Firth and conducted by Howard Rooke.

Later still in March, I was at Christ Church, Ipswich, performing with other soloists unknown to me, in a work entitled *Calvary*. The conductor was, as ever in our Ipswich performances, Gordon Hawkins.

Another *Crucifixion*, this time at Fakenham Parish Church, added yet another digit to the number of times I have sung in this work so revered by Church choirs, on this occasion sung by Fakenham Musical Society. Brian Ellum was organist and Bill Purchase conducted.

Audrey and I were at Starston Parish Church in May, singing with Rita Green and Richard White in another performance of Mendelssohn's *Elijah*.

Following a successful presentation of the *Beggar's Opera'* last year in the new Sewell Barn Theatre, we chose Martinu's *The Marriage* and Gilbert and Sullivan's *Trial By Jury*.

We had presented *The Marriage* on two previous occasions, one at the Maddermarket Theatre and one (the 'outer-space' version) at Cromer Pier. This time we reverted to a straightforward realisation of Martinu's opera, which is based on a one-act play by Gogol, and set in nineteenth century St Petersburgh. This work is great fun, and is among my most memorable experiences of days with Norfolk Opera Players. Only Audrey and I had acted in all three presentations of this work.

We were with the Fakenham Choral Society again in late November to perform in Bach's *Christmas Oratorio* with an orchestra led by Norman Moor and conducted by Bill Purchase.

Ten choirs of the East Anglian Federation of Townswomen's Guilds combined to present a *Festival of Carols* at St Peter Mancroft Church. Valerie Walker and I were soloists, Kenneth Ryder accompanied and Mary Firth conducted. On this occasion, the programme reminds me, I was also narrator in Schutz's *The Christmas Story*, whilst Valerie Walker sang the soprano solos.

To end this year's serious musical undertakings, I sang with Alison Humphreys in a performance of Brahms' *Requiem* with the Great Yarmouth Musical Society at the Town Hall. The orchestra was led by Colin Clouting and conducted by Gregory Underwood.

Yes, we ended the year at the Maddermarket. As I recall it, we always performed a matinée on Boxing Day followed by an evening performance, and were regaled with fish and chips in the time between.

Chapter 34 - 1981

The Creation (Fakenham Church) ~ *Merry Wives of Windsor*
(St Andrew's Hall, Norwich) ~ Jane Manning's Recital (Assembly House,
Norwich) ~ *Messiah* (Cromer Church) ~ Dvorak's *Stabat Mater*
(Yarmouth Town Hall) ~ *The Prima Donna's Mother is a Drag*
(Sewell Barn Theatre, Norwich) ~ Fauré's *Requiem* and
Bach's *Magnificat* (St John's Catholic Cathedral, Norwich)

Having performed Martinu's *The Marriage* for the third time in 1980, we seemed
to be thinking in triplicate, because we now presented Nicolai's *The Merry Wives
of Windsor* for the third time, on this occasion at St Andrew's Hall.

In choosing an opera for performance I always observed four criteria:

1. Good chorus work.
2. Orchestral work that could be well presented with the small number of
   rehearsals that could be accorded the players.
3. Ability to cast the opera within our own ranks.
4. Box office appeal.

This last criterion was the most difficult to meet, since we had pledged
ourselves not to try to compete with the professional companies who toured the
more well known works.

Our previous presentations of *The Merry Wives* had met with considerable
acclaim, the last one at this time quite a distant memory to us and to our local
opera-going supporters. Audrey was still cast as Mrs Page, and this time I was
Mr Page instead of Mr Ford as previously. Dennis Johnson was musical director.
He had acted often enough as assistant to Fred Firth, who had directed several
of our previous presentations, and I thought it was time for Dennis to be his own
man. He acquitted himself well.

In glancing at the back page of this programme, I observe the following
advertisement: - 'AUDREY YATES (Hand crafted suede and leather)
(Instructor for Norfolk Education Committee and Norfolk Federation of
Women's Institutes)'. This was Audrey's venture into business (taking Ros
Wilkinson as a partner) after leaving her post as Crafts Organiser for the
Disabled – but this is another story.

Our old friend Jane Manning, having become one of the most distinguished
exponents of contemporary music, sang in the 30th anniversary Concert of the
Norfolk and Norwich Music Club on Saturday 4th April at the Assembly House.
My archives show that I was singing in a *Messiah* at Cromer Parish Church on
that day, so that I could not have been present at Jane's recital.

Margaret Norden and I were soloists for Dvorak's *Stabat Mater* at Yarmouth
Town Hall on 13th April. This was the first time I had sung with Margaret, a
very pleasant experience.

My researches into small operas resulted in our presenting *The Prima Donna's Mother is a Drag* by Donizetti, recently revived by Opera Rara, who were founded in 1970 to revive unjustly neglected operatic works of the 19th century. When Opera Rara first performed this work in 1972, the critics hailed it as 'the funniest opera of all times'. I think we made our audience laugh, too. The production was in the hands of Norma Wick, with musical direction and accompaniment by Eileen Last.

This small opera was coupled with an Offenbach opera entitled *Paquerette*. This was produced by Roy Emerson, with the musical direction and accompaniment by Judy Tovey. This was Roy's first involvement with opera production for Norfolk Opera Player's, and he acquitted himself most admirably in this capacity.

Bach's *Magnificat* at St John's Catholic Cathedral involved Audrey. Bob Arnett was singing the bass solos, and other contributors were Alison Humphreys, Ann Moore, and Richard White. St. John's is not an easy place to sing in, with its excessive acoustical properties, particularly when stationed under the tower, but all contributors sang well. The performance was by Norwich Singers under the baton of Dennis Johnson. I think that this was the occasion that I was able to organise the conveyance of Norfolk Opera Players' scenery flats as a background to the singers. I believe that they helped.

The year's engagements appear to have ended early this year with a performance in July of *The Creation*. The soprano soloist on this occasion was Kathleen Ahearn. She was the wife of Randall Baker, who at that time was a lecturer at the University of East Anglia. I mention this because, in his role of orator at the University of East Anglia honorary degrees ceremony (possibly in this year, or maybe next) he invited Audrey and me to attend in order to accompany Dame Alicia Markova, famous ballerina, while she sat waiting for her honorary doctorate degree to be awarded. She was with her sister, and proved to be a most attractive and modest woman, as was her sister also.

Chapter 35 - 1982

Elgar's *Coronation Ode* (Gresham's School, Holt) ~ *Captain Noah and His Floating Zoo* and excerpts from *HMS Pinafore* (Woodbridge) ~ *The Creation* (St John's Roman Catholic Cathedral, Norwich) ~ *Elijah* (Cromer Church) ~ Fauré's *Requiem* (St Nicholas Chapel, King's Lynn) ~ *The Gurney Girl* (Triennial Festival, Theatre Royal, Norwich) ~ Concert (Poringland Church) ~ *Messiah* (The Citadel, Norwich) ~ *Messiah* excerpts (Eaton (CNS) School) ~ Maddermarket Music Hall.

The first concert of the year was at Gresham's School – a performance, amongst other items, by the school choir, of Elgar's *Coronation Ode*. Sir Edward Elgar was commissioned by the management of Covent Garden Opera House to write this ode in celebration of the 1902 Coronation. It includes the famous tune from the trio section of the Pomp and Circumstance March No.1, which Elgar proudly claimed, and rightly, would 'knock 'em flat'. Edward V11 himself had suggested to him that he should have words written to this tune, and the Eton housemaster, A.C. Benson, provided them. Contrary to fashionable belief, Elgar (and his librettist) was no flag-waving jingoist, and this work, while fairly distant from the spiritual heights of *Gerontius*, is occasional music of the best kind.

I was joined on this occasion by soloists Alison Humphreys, Elizabeth Gould and Richard White. The conductor was Richard Peaver.

In May, Gordon Hawkins asked me to sing the solos in *Captain Noah and his Floating Zoo* (words by Michael Flanders, music by Joseph Horovitz), and also in a concert performance of *HMS Pinafore*. This took place in Woodbridge cinema and was presented by Woodbridge Choral Society. *Captain Noah* is a pleasant, light-hearted work, which I had previously performed for John Barnett at Thorpe High School (although I have no programme of this occasion which consequently does not feature in these memoirs). The items in which I was involved were taken at a very smart tempo. Imagine my surprise therefore when Gordon chose tempi about half those of my Thorpe renditions. *HMS Pinafore* was not very exciting either.

Audrey was with me, because we had been staying in Kent with Julia, awaiting the arrival of her first baby. We had to leave before it arrived, because of the Woodbridge concert. The week before our visit to Julia, we had lost our Great Dane dog (an emotional episode). Upon our return home we found that our bungalow had been burgled. The place was in a mess, but a £30 silver collection for Lizzy's children was the only thing taken. We recovered the amount from insurance. The next day, Julia's first born, Jay, arrived.

Creation came next in June, in St John's Roman Catholic Cathedral. The acoustics had not improved, but I believe that The Norwich Singers, Alison Humphreys, Richard White and I, together with full orchestra (leader Leonard Callaway, conductor Dennis Johnson), gave of our best.

Elijah again at Cromer in July, with the Sheringham and Cromer Choral Society, conducted by Howard Rooke with Clive Jones at the organ, added to the number of oratorio performances in which we had been involved over the past thirty-odd years.

I sang in Fauré's *Requiem* with the King's Lynn Festival Chorus, as part of their annual music festival. After the performance, I was introduced to the famous mezzo-soprano Janet Baker. A rather formal affair.

This was the year of the Norwich Triennial Festival again. Audrey and I had been involved over the years, with Antony Hopkins' massive works, requiring massed school choirs and orchestras. One or two soloists were usually employed and we had been fortunate enough to contribute to these productions. This year it was to be a work by Douglas Coombes, entitled *The Gurney Girl* to be performed at the Theatre Royal. Douglas had of course been a musical director of Norfolk Opera Players before moving to London to take up an appointment with the BBC, presenting children's programmes.

In *The Gurney Girl*, Douglas's wife Carole played the leading role. The libretto was by David Self, and the production was in the hands of Hubert Mitchell. My role was that of Handsome Johnny (no derisory remarks please), father of Elizabeth (later to become Elizabeth Fry) and the other Gurney girls. Audrey was originally cast in a part that she didn't enjoy, and conceded this to someone else.

David Self's libretto involved many characters, including several branches of the Gurney dynasty, staff and prisoners of Newgate Prison, children of the prisoners, urchins and imps. The sheer numbers involved and the individual performances of a large cast presented Hubert with a hefty undertaking, and I think he made the most of it.

It was a pleasure to be again performing with children (in spite of that old maxim about performing with children or dogs). My own grandchildren were there, and distinguished themselves, though not so much for their thespian excellence. In the case of Luke, it was a certain unwillingness to rehearse. Our rehearsal venue was the Hewett School and Luke had to be prised away from ball-games in the playground. In the case of Melissa it was an over-willingness to make her mark, which included trying to seduce Douglas Coombes with siren glances (she was six). Anyway she managed to make the most of the three words she was called upon to utter, and after the final curtain Luke managed to position himself in the foreground for a photograph with the American ambassador, who had come to see the show.

Another illustrious person was also present, the Duchess of York, to whom I was introduced. She was charming.

Norma Wick asked me to join her and Margaret Elliott and Keith Wincote, in a concert at Poringland Church (Norma's home ground). Also listed were Jeanne and Len, and I'm sorry that I cannot remember details of their contribution, although I am sure their contribution was of a high standard.

Another *Messiah*, this time at the Salvation Army's Citadel, and excerpts from the *Messiah* at my old school (City of Norwich) completed the year's serious work, with the inevitable Maddermarket Music Hall light-heartedly anticipating the New Year.

This was a memorable year because it brought to a close my administration and chairmanship of Norfolk Opera Players which Audrey and I had founded twenty years previously. I was quoted in the Press as saying, 'twenty years is enough'. That statement about summed it up. For those twenty years I had never been free of the planning and organisation of operas, an achievement of which I was proud, but the accomplishment of which had invaded every waking hour. I handed my successor a fourteen-page document on the history and management of Norfolk Opera Players. Jeffrey Davies was my successor. He was not a member of NOP but had presented his credentials to me earlier, as a producer and singer. There were other NOP members interested in taking over, but knowing the complexities of running an opera company, I saw in Jeffrey the qualities which were needed, and by a democratic vote at the Annual General Meeting he was elected.

Since that time, others have succeeded Jeffrey in the role of Chairman, and various musical directors and producers have been engaged. Some degree of permanence has existed in recent years by the continuing engagement as Musical Director of Patricia Clouting, wife of the talented Colin Clouting mentioned in earlier notes, and of course renowned in her own right.

**After the farewell party from the Norfolk Opera Players,
with Audrey and Colin Thackery**

Chapter 36 - 1983

Messiah (Gresham's School, Holt) ~ *Elijah* (Norwich Cathedral) ~
Doctor Miracle (Sewell Barn Theatre, Norwich) ~ Recital (Thurne
Methodist Chapel) ~ Maddermarket Music Hall.

We were at Gresham's again in March, singing in Handel's *Messiah* once more. We didn't really need our books by this time, but traditionally one holds the vocal score. Other soloists were Alison Humphreys and Richard White. The conductor was again Richard Peaver, and the leader of the orchestra Peter Detron. Reference to the programme reveals that the chorus numbered 61, which, apart from Gresham pupils included those from Beeston Hall School, Norwich High School and Runton Hall. Quite a few of the sopranos and contraltos are listed as 'Mrs', presumably mothers or teachers, and similarly some of the tenors' and basses' names are complemented by 'Mr' prefixes.

The biggest thing in 1983 was a staged presentation of Mendelssohn's oratorio *Elijah* in Norwich Cathedral. This was the production we had spoken of in that Docking pub, and which we had been rehearsing in 1982.

'In this work, the composer unfolds the personal drama of the life of the great prophet with such dramatic impact that it cries out for a fully staged, costumed production'. These were the words of Richard White, endorsed by many, including Dennis Johnson and myself. We three, in fact, formed a triumvirate, Richard (producer) Dennis (musical director) and myself (administrator) to launch this enterprise. The success or the venture however would be dependent upon the excellence of many people whose expertise and dedication would be in great demand. How fortunate we were in attracting those creative people. Stage lighting (again by means of additional lighting brought in through a clerestory window) was the preserve of Robert Forster and others with steeplejack proclivities. Stage construction at the west end was under the supervision of Gordon Marshall and John Gray, with Bush Builders supplying and erecting scaffolding. Costumes were designed by Helen Hoyte and realised by Joan Thackery and team from old sheets and discarded clothing. Costumes and properties were designed to complement Mendelssohn's musical vision of the story rather than to reflect historical veracity.

The statue of Baal (18ft high) on a 6ft high pedestal, was designed by Brian Hartley, made of steel rods surrounded by wire netting and papier mâché made from copies of the *Financial Times* provided by a friend of Brian, and judiciously draped in the day-time in deference to Cathedral worshippers and visitors. I could go on, but I think it would take as much space to list every individual (although deserving of such mention) as to reproduce extracts from the programme, which I append at the end of this narrative.

Richard had decided to let the great Norman building work for him as a setting for this story of Elijah's struggle with Baal and his servant Jezebel for the souls of the Jewish people. Therefore no scenery was used, but the Norwich City

Chief Engineer was most co-operative in arranging to floodlight the west window externally.

We were of course extremely grateful to the Dean and Chapter for giving us permission to stage this event, and we were particularly indebted to George Alison, sacrist and also a friend, for his collaboration and assistance in the staging and presentation. I wonder whether he knew that when 'the fire descended from heaven', it would be by means of a calor gas cylinder, relaying gas to a contrivance of Bill Bailey, and switched on at the appropriate moment by Colin Thackery, producing a flame reaching almost to the triforium.

Richard had always wanted me to sing the part of Elijah, having sung in the oratorio so many times and in so many places, more often than not with Richard singing the tenor role. And so it was decided that I should be cast in that role, and that we should invite singers to audition for the other characters. Naturally I was pleased when Audrey was chosen as the Angel (type-casting of course). Others chosen completed a strong cast, and response to advertising for chorus and acting members was very productive.

Two ballet companies were to be involved, Margot Warne choreographing the Norwich Ballet Club to depict the Angelic dancers, and Janice Sinclair choreographing the Crome Centre Modern Dance Group as the Baal dancers. These two ballet clubs, together with sixty-five singers and actors provided a company of about 100 performers on stage.

Having sung together with Audrey in *Elijah* with many Norfolk and Suffolk choral societies, I invited the societies of Great Yarmouth, Sheringham and Cromer, Lowestoft and the Norwich Singers to join, book in hand and sing from the South side of the stage. Norwich Singers (Dennis was their M.D.) and Lowestoft Choral Society responded and, following a Press notice I think, so did the students of Diss High School. The orchestra was to be conducted by Dennis Johnson, experienced in choral and opera conducting, and also a musician of rare ability, proficient in playing piano, violin, and brass instruments ranging from trumpet to tuba.

The orchestra of 40 players, led by Frederick Firth were placed on the North side of the stage inside the west door, and closed circuit television monitors were used to obtain contact between performers and off-stage chorus. The disposition of the orchestra was such that it enabled the entry to the stage of singers proceeding from the north transept. This was a delicate operation in view of the small space available and I am told that a trombonist made more than one adjustment to the musical score as a result.

There were of course, other difficulties. Audrey, as the Angel, had to spend the whole performance standing in the extremely narrow gallery at aisle roof level. Negotiating the stairway was tricky enough. More so was the attaining of the central position, accomplished by chasséing sideways, the magnitude of her wings precluding any more straightforward approach. Mark you, before Audrey took up her position (in very subdued lighting) I had had to position myself there for my opening declamation. But I had no wings to contend with.

In the second half of the performance nine other angels (five female, four male) had to insinuate themselves along the gallery, one of them, I am told, rather averse to heights, having to indulge in a little nicotine before venturing up the access stairway and across to the north side, where, later in the performances, they were required to sing (and quite beautifully they did it) the two pieces normally allocated to the quartet of soloists in an oratorio performance. There were no casualties that I knew of in a situation that would have been rather unkind to anyone suffering an attack of 'angelic vertigo'. The frail metal parapet of the 26 feet high gallery is a mere three feet high.

The whole venture proved to be a great success, an epic occasion which people who saw it talk about to this day. We had a dress rehearsal on the Monday, and gave five performances. We had to turn people away on the Saturday, and I believe we could have attracted audiences for another week. Truly a triumph for the incomparable Richard, and for Dennis, and for everyone who either acted or sang, or contributed their skills and time to enable the presentation to take place. Special mention must be made here of the indefatigable Margaret Johnson, who played piano for all rehearsals which started in 1982, and continued to the week of presentation. Margaret had been, and was afterwards, an accompanist on whom we had relied for many a recital and teaching occasion.

Elijah (Robert Yates) and Obadiah (Brian Tuffrey)

137

eLijah '83 society

Producer & Stage Director	Richard White
Musical Director & Conductor	Dennis Johnson
Administrator	Robert Yates
Secretary & Treasurer	Jenny Newark
Choreographer/Director of Norwich Ballet Club (Angelic Dancers)	Margot Warne
Choreographer of The Crome Centre Modern Dance Group (Dancers of Baal)	Janice Sinclair
Lighting Designer	Robert Forster
Rehearsal pianist and lighting cues	Margaret Johnson
Costumes designer	Helen Hoyte
Costumes realised by	Joan Thackery assisted by Jan Greenland, Linda Aspland, Bridget Bullivant and members of the society
Stage construction and management	Gordon Marshall, John Gray and friends
Statue of Baal	Sculpture by Brian Hartley and Angela Galey-Jones in Ros Newman's group at Wensum Lodge.
Base of Baal Statue	Varnham Lightowler, Colin Thackery
Thrones built by	Mick McCord
Menorah made by	Peter Staniland
Properties	Ian Sinclair and Richard White
Make-up	Liz Hillman and team
Poster design	Godfrey Arnison
Ticket Secretaries	Sheila Corner, Mary Gogle
Call-boy	Catherine Snook
Property Mistresses	Molly Turner, Chantal Riches

cast

ELIJAH	Robert Yates
OBADIAH	Brian Tuffrey
AN ANGEL	Audrey Yates
THE WIDOW	Kathleen Chapman
AHAB	Robert Arnett
ISRAELITE WOMAN	Ann Moore
HEBREW BOY	Jacob White
ISRAELITE WOMAN	Ann Youngman
QUEEN JEZEBEL	Sally Stock
AN ANGEL	Sybil Kent

DUET (with Chorus): 'Lord, Bow Thine Ear to my prayer'	Margaret Gallant, Kay Holmes
TRIO: 'Life Thine Eyes'	Lucy White, Jacob White, Christian White
ANGELS	Sylvia Bailey, Sybil Snelling, Janet Arnett, Susan Gee, Judy Reid, Vernon Holt, Christopher Speake, Maurice Bird, Trevor Thurston
ANGELIC DANCERS (members of the Norwich Ballet Club)	Janet Aldham, Caroline Ashbolt, Janice Baker, Susie Harrison, Marigold Hyde-Smith, Diana Jiminez, Eileen Pennington, Donna Smith, Helen Visick, Joyce Wiseman, Stella Wiseman
DANCERS OF BAAL (members of the Crome Centre Modern Dance Group)	Janice Sinclair, Gillian Atterson, Jennifer Bugg, Rosemary Clarke, Janice Edye, Debbie Katra, Sandra Mould

138

ORCHESTRA

1st VIOLINS   Frederick Firth (Leader), Ken Boast, Len Callaway, Thelma Cooke, Eileen Pearce, Nora Pearson
2nd VIOLINS   Ian Gray, Kathie Bass, Geoffrey Foote, Beryl Gray, John Lobel
VIOLAS   Wendy Ward, Sian Evans, Jean Langdale-Pope, Beverley Rogers, Janet West
CELLOS   Ursula Pank, Mary Pilkington, Peter Shaw, Jemma Sidell
DOUBLE BASSES   Colin Goodchild, Joseph Mason
FLUTES   Michael Butcher, Michael Bass
OBOES   John Rose, Christine Coverdale
CLARINETS   Roger West, Roger Miller
BASSOONS   Ian Summers, Glyn Thomas
HORNS   Barbara Houlston, Neville Thrower, Rachel Tooley, Joanna Ede
TRUMPETS   David Brooke, Mary Mandilakis
TROMBONES   Tony Spurrell, Elaine McCash (except Wednesday) Derrick Wick (Wednesday only), John Sheppard
TYPANI   Andrew Gibson
ORGAN   Malcolm Archer

The Baal Dancers

139

Sybil Kent (an Angel) was suffering from a bad cold – definitely non-U with angels. Sylvia Bailey, substituted and right angelically did she sing.

In July Norfolk Opera Players invaded the Sewell Barn theatre again and presented *Amelia Goes to the Ball*, a one-act opera by Menotti, and *Doctor Miracle* by Bizet, also a one-acter in which I played the part of the Mayor of Padua. The comic theme of the plot centres on a romance between Lauretta and Silvio, who appears in various disguises to outwit Lauretta's father, the Mayor and her stepmother. An allegedly poisoned omelette adds to the complications. (How much easier it is to explain the plot of these one-act operas, than to attempt to summarise the intricacies of most grand operas, when you inevitably find yourself 'on a loser').

We were at Thurne again later in the year (one-sheet programme undated). It seems that we were on our own (even the pianist's name is not mentioned) singing about ten songs each.

I have no record of Maddermarket Music Hall in this year and subsequent years, so I must assume that last year marked the end of our contributions to that yearly activity. I know that for some years now we had asked to be released – not because we didn't enjoy it, but felt it was better to move on before we became stale. Our earlier request to go had been reluctantly accepted by Ian Emmerson, with the proviso that we would come again in an emergency. There had been an emergency for the last five years.

I do recall a certain feeling of freedom on Boxing Day and New Year's Eve in being able to choose one's method of celebration – a sort of renaissance.

***Elijah*: Audrey and other Angels**

140

Chapter 37 - 1984

Chandos Anthem No.6 and Haydn's *Nelson Mass* (St John's Roman Catholic Cathedral, Norwich) ~ Brahms' *Requiem* (Gresham's School, Holt) ~ Concert (Buxton Church) ~ Norwich Sing for Pleasure Festival (compère and adjudicator) ~ *Festival of Carols* (St Peter Mancroft Church, Norwich)

I appear not to have a programme of the first event listed above, but I remember the occasion, if only for the fact that Handel's *Chandos Anthem No. 6* contains music for the contralto voice (undoubtedly originally for the castrato) which is so low in the stave that few contraltos would be able to project it in the cavernous resonance of St. John's Catholic Cathedral. Audrey was one of those contraltos who could.

Without a programme, I cannot tell you with whom we performed in Haydn's *Nelson Mass*.

In March I was again at Gresham's, performing with Alison Humphreys, in Brahms' *Requiem*. Also in the programme was Brahms' *Alto Rhapsody*, sung by Elizabeth Gould.

At Buxton Church in June, Audrey and I joined Phillip and Kathie Chapman and Richard White in a concert entitled 'Music for a Summer Evening', a title which graced our contributions of English songs, duets, quartets and excerpts from Mendelssohn's *Elijah*. The programme does not reveal who accompanied us.

In July, ten choirs from all over England came to St. Andrews Hall to sing and compete, in a programme entitled 'Norwich Sing for Pleasure Festival'. The event attracted ten choirs totalling 200 singers. 'Sing for Pleasure' is a national organisation that promotes choral singing, especially among young people. The Norwich concert was arranged by Andrew Piersenné who asked me to come along and adjudicate, together with a lady who I think was connected in some way with the organisation. In addition to adjudicating, I found myself having to arrange the disposition of the singers from the many choirs, so as to enable them to come downstage and perform and then return to their seats with the minimum of fuss. I think I did a pretty good job and quite quickly. The choirs all sang extremely well but we chose the Skelmanthorpe Male Voice Choir (Huddersfield) as the winners.

Valerie Walker and I were soloists in a *Festival of Carols* at St Peter Mancroft, presented by the Combined Guild Choirs of the East Anglian Federation of Townswomen's Guilds. Ten Guild choirs took part. I was also Narrator, the organist was Kenneth Ryder and the conductor the indefatigable Mary Firth.

This was the year in which I started to teach singing. Audrey had launched herself into this activity some years earlier, and in spite of my reservations about the wisdom of this venture, she was making a good job of it, as a singing tutor to Adult Education classes at Drayton and Hellesdon. A vacancy occurred for a singing tutor to such a class at Fakenham, and, urged on by Audrey, I was successful in being appointed. The venue initially was a mobile classroom at Fakenham High School, and later a room at the Middle School where the headmaster, David Stapleford, who had already enrolled in the singing class, was to provide accommodation for the next eight years. David is a most likeable and reliable man, loves singing, and was to become a regular member of our singing classes for years to come.

Feeling a certain presumptuousness initially, I satisfied my conscience in the knowledge that Audrey and I had enjoyed so much singing, and such variety that it would good to endeavour to pass some of our knowledge, experience and acquired technique to others.

NORWICH SING FOR PLEASURE FESTIVAL

7th JULY '84

Chapter 38 - 1985

Elgar's *Coronation Ode* (Gresham's School, Holt) ~ *Olivet to Calvary* (St Remigius Church, Hethersett) ~ Raymond Warren's *In the Beginning* (Norwich Cathedral) ~ Concert at Thurne ~ Maddermarket Music Hall

I was commissioned to sing in Elgar's *Coronation Ode* (for the second time) at Gresham's School. Audrey and I had contributed to quite a number of performances at Gresham's and had enjoyed them, particularly since we were always regaled with supper afterwards! We had also enjoyed empathy with the several musical directors over the years, the most recent incumbent of that office being the efficient and likeable Richard Peaver.

Nevertheless I began to feel that we had performed with choral societies in Norfolk and Suffolk so many times, that it was time to fade out of this activity. Therefore, when asked to sing in Brahms' *Requiem* the following year, I declined and recommended that Bob Arnett should take my place. This proved to be quite a critical move, particularly since I so enjoy the baritone solos in Brahms' *Requiem*.

This action, I think, effectively terminated a period stretching from 1948, during which time Audrey and I had been contralto and bass (or baritone) soloists in so many works with so many societies. The bush telegraph had obviously operated to tell the world that 'Bob and Audrey had had enough'. It wasn't quite the end however, as the following years' events will reveal.

A concert was arranged to celebrate the 75th anniversary of the foundation of the City of Norwich School. I was an old boy of that school, having entered by means of a county scholarship, but cannot claim to have performed exceptionally well thereafter. I was asked by Colin Goodchild to contribute to the concert. Colin, at this time, had been Head of Music at the school from 1968, and consequently was in charge of providing orchestra, choir and soloists.

The programme shows that Colin recruited a choir of 118 singers, an orchestra of 48 players, and a wind band of 61 players. The tenors and basses in the choir were mostly ex-pupils, but a few others swelled their ranks, including staff and ex-staff. The City of Norwich School is now a mixed school, but for many years had been a boys' school. Recruitment of ex-pupils of the feminine gender therefore was not so productive, so parents, friends, staff and ex-staff augmented the ranks of the sopranos and contraltos.

The choir sang two unaccompanied part-songs, and two Negro spirituals. Then they presented, with orchestra, excerpts from Haydn's *Creation*. This is where I was involved, in singing the bass solos, together with Sybil Snelling, soprano and previously a teacher at the school, and Roger Elias, tenor, ex-pupil and now a general practitioner. The bass contributions included the aria 'Now heaven in fullest glory' which I so enjoy singing. It was a memorable occasion for all performers, and, I believe, for audience also.

My old friend Duncan Pigg recruited me to sing in a performance of *Olivet to Calvary* (J.H Maunder) at St Remigius Church, Hethersett, where he was choir-master. I sang in the company of Philip Tuckwood, tenor, Barbara Powell, soprano and Roger Mapes, baritone. The organist was Peter Onslow and Duncan Pigg conducted. The Hethersett Methodist Church Choir, the Humbleyard Singers, some friends and members of Hethersett W.I. Choir and Hethersett Musical Society, augmented the church choir.

In October, in the 47th Norfolk and Norwich Festival of Music and the Arts, I again became involved with one of the Festival's productions; an opera of two acts entitled *In the Beginning*. This was a musical composition by Raymond Warren using words from Genesis and Paradise Lost.

Following the tradition of the Festival, it was a large-scale work with chorus, orchestra and on this occasion hand-bell ringers, all recruited from schools, colleges and the University of East Anglia, together with dancers from the Norwich Schools of Dancing. To qualify my use of the description 'large-scale', let me give numbers involved. Choir members totalled 177, orchestra 71, hand-bell ringers 14, dancers 29, all this presented on a specially constructed stage at the west end of Norwich Cathedral. In addition, were the principal characters of God, Adam, Eve, Satan and the Son of God.

The director and producer was Andy Smith, then of Maddermarket renown, the musical director Michael Nicholas, and the organist Adrian Lucas. The orchestra was tutored by John Burdett, and sectional tutoring given by six of the county's well known and accomplished musicians.

A pupil of mine, Lorna Stapleford, had auditioned for the role of Eve, and had been accepted, sharing the role with another girl, Nancy Fraser. Lorna sang very well, and justified not only her own selection, but also my own reputation, since the programme listed me as singing coach.

Raymond Warren may not be such a household name as some of our modern English composers, but he had, before 1985, written two symphonies, a violin concerto, three string quartets and six operas. The original commission for *In the Beginning* was for the International Society for Music Education Festival, and was staged in the Roman Catholic Cathedral in Clifton.

The singer cast in the role of God, then and now, was Michael Rippon, well-known international baritone, and a professor of music and singing at Hong Kong University. Michael Nicholas had sometime earlier asked if I would understudy the part. I accepted, and I took my commission seriously, because it was an extremely difficult modern work written in manuscript in typical composer's script.

The performances were scheduled for the 17th, 18th, (2.30 pm and 7.30 pm) and 19th October. On the morning of the 17th, Roger Rowe, who was administrator and co-ordinator, phoned to say that Michael had arrived, but that he had contracted Hong Kong 'flu – could I take the afternoon dress rehearsal and evening performance? Well, I had had one run-through a week or so earlier in case of an emergency. The emergency had presented itself. I sang the whole of my Act 1 music from the gallery in front of the west window, twenty-six feet up, as I had done in the opening declarations in Mendelssohn's *Elijah* back in 1983.

Musical entries were all difficult, since the orchestration gave no assistance. One had to be confident of pitching one's note against the orchestra's representation of the creation. A sign from the musical director would assist one's correct entry. At dress rehearsal, this was achieved. In the evening performance, Satan came in at stage level amidst a cloud of dry ice, blotting out the conductor, except for the finger of his left hand. You have to have good nerves to be a soloist - you also have to have good luck. Good luck prevailed.

Roger Rowe 'phoned in the morning to say that Michael was still suffering, so would I take the matinée performance? I did, and Michael sang in the evening performance, controlling his cold sufficiently to put in a good performance. In his earlier performance at Bristol, he had been given acting instructions. These instructions were limited to expressive use of the arms and hands. I mention this because I was not given any instruction, and, as a result, had decided that, as God, it would be appropriate to remain statuesque, relying on vocal authority to effect the Creation of the World in seven days.

In the morning, Roger Rowe 'phoned again. In the evening's final performance, 'would I sing the part of God, if Michael mimed it?' He was still suffering and his performance had not helped his recovery. This was an amazing suggestion, but I said that I would do anything to save the show. It showed great faith in me of course, and I was duly flattered, but I said we would have to consult Michael Nicholas to see if he thought this would be possible. We cornered him where he was rehearsing the orchestra in the north transept. Though alarmed at the suggestion, he said that this might be possible in Act 1, which was sung from the gallery, but would never work at ground floor stage level in Acts II and III. Our joint final resolution was that Michael would sing, and that I would stand hidden behind the pillar at the south side of the gallery, ready to break forth if Michael's voice gave out. Our voices were remarkably similar, and since we were of the same height and build, there had been no problems with the robes. He had even used my sandals.

If his voice gave out, I would probably have to give the odd peep round the pillar to see the conductor's beat. To be as inconspicuous as possible, I borrowed the Dean's black cloak. Happily Michael's voice didn't let him down. On my way afterwards to disrobe, I passed the organist and a group of lay clerks, and explained that I had been acting as the Holy Ghost, a statement well received by the group. Michael Rippon had confided in me that it had been essential for him to put in at least two performances in order to collect some of his fee to pay for his air flight back to Hong Kong. His fee was a substantial one, and I was pleased to collect part of it.

My earlier mention of acting instruction was necessary in order to regale you with the following anecdote. It is always an activity of schoolchildren at these functions to ask for autographs, and this was no exception. They produce all sorts of scraps of paper, and one does one's best to accommodate them. One of the children on this occasion said to me: 'We like you betteran 'im, 'e move about too much'.

Another item worthy of mention is that after one of the performances, Audrey and I took our two grandchildren (who had attended the performance)

145

to the Odeon cinema. The audience was a very small one. After the film, a little girl came down from the back of the cinema with her parents, saw me, and said, 'Excuse me, I'm not mistaken, am I?' 'No,' I replied, 'I'm God'. She of course had been in one of the performances.

Finally, let me say that in advertising for a pianist to accompany my singing tuition, a young man responded, and was so accomplished that I immediately accepted him. He then told me that he had been in one of the school choirs performing in *In the Beginning* and said that my voice was the first real baritone voice that he had heard. He has now been assisting for about six years, and his playing and his personality have been of incomparable value to me. His name is **Christian Stirling.**

***In the Beginning* at Norwich Cathedral**

Chapter 39 - 1986

No list is required for this year, since my records reveal only one programmed performance.

I like to think that the situation was the result of the musical 'grapevine' spreading the news of our desire to reduce commitments.

Anyway, our one performance was with the King's Lynn Festival Chorus Society, who presented Mozart's *Requiem Mass* and Charpentier's *Te Deum*. The Cantata Orchestra led by Christopher Finch accompanied them. The conductor was David Steel (No! not that one) and other soloists joining Audrey and myself were soprano Alison Humphreys and tenor Michael Morris.

**Dr Miracle (Robert Yates) with Janet Arnett (left) and
Susan Morris (right)at the Sewell Barn. See page 135**

Chapter 40 - 1987

Olivet to Calvary (St Gregory's Church, Norwich) ~ *Elijah* (Norwich Cathedral) ~ Fauré's *Requiem* (St Margaret's Church, Old Catton) ~ A Celebration of Christmas Music (St Margaret's Church, King's Lynn) ~ *Christmas Oratorio* (Fakenham Church)

Despite 1986, my involvement with Choral Societies was not yet over, as evidenced by the performances listed above.

The tenor soloist in *Olivet to Cavalry* was Brian Tuffrey, the accompanist Olive Lee, and the conductor Mary Firth. And for what other reason would Mary have been there than that the performance was being presented by the East Anglian Federation of Townswomen's Guilds?

In June, Michael Nicholas invited me to sing *Elijah* with the Norwich Philharmonic Society. I think that Audrey and I are perhaps the only husband and wife who have each performed as soloists with the Philharmonic Society. The other soloists were all professional and it is a point of interest that the tenor soloist, Neill Archer, was also taking this role in a performance of *Elijah*, which our daughter Elizabeth invited us to see at Birmingham Symphony Hall a few years later.

Although I have never been a member of the Townswomen's Guild (honestly!) I seem to have been part of their performances over a number of years. Again, therefore, at Catton with the local branch of that worthy society, I sang the baritone solos in Fauré's *Requiem*, and also contributed 'Watchful's Song', from Vaughan Williams' *Pilgrim's Progress*.

I haven't finished yet, for 'A Celebration of Christmas Music' at St Margaret's Church, King's Lynn, was presented by the Beccles, Catton, Lowestoft, King's Lynn, Earlham, Lakenham and Wensum combined choirs of the East Anglian Federation of Townswomen's Guilds, conductor Mary Firth, accompanist Aubrey Hood, soprano Catherine Kirke. I think that my contribution must have been made in a cantata entitled *Night of Miracles* by J. Peterson.

Finally, and this substantially marked the end of our performances with Choral Societies, the Fakenham Musical Society asked me to sing the bass solos in Bach's *Christmas Oratorio*. I have used the word 'substantially' because Audrey and I were, some ten years later to perform in a *Messiah*. But I will come to this in due course.

Chapter 41 – 1947-1987

I think that Audrey and I have been extremely privileged to have been invited to sing in so many performances, in so many places, and with so many Choral Societies. The fact that we have been in equal demand has, I am sure, enabled us to pursue this interest in both its semi-professional and amateur directions.

Perhaps it wouldn't be too irrelevant here to say that we have shared most other interests, including extensive gardening operations, many home alterations, including adding an additional 800 square feet – all 'hands on'.

I think that I have not been too successful in an anecdotal sense in cataloguing performances with choral societies. The fact is that these engagements were professional, giving little opportunity for contact with members, apart from the occasional 'bun-struggle' after the performance. Even then we would be anxious to get home because of tomorrow's working day, and in earlier years, to our parental duties. Our involvement with the musical aspect was totally absorbing, requiring no anecdotal episode to stir the memory.

However, it is difficult to recall how hard we must have striven to learn new works, with only one afternoon rehearsal before evening performance, arriving by motor-cycle or unreliable car, then to change after the afternoon rehearsal into one's tail-suit, with starched shirt front in the earlier days. This required much diligence and ability to suffer pain in inserting all the studs where they had to go, quite often needing to invoke Audrey's assistance. Tails, to my mind, never looked so smart after fashion dictated that the shirt front should be soft, and the wing collar replaced with a turn-down one.

In listing performances, I have tried to give names to other principal participants without making this document too much of a catalogue. There has always been a danger of this. Undoubtedly I shall have failed in not giving sufficient recognition to some individuals, and perhaps of failing to mention others. Additionally, of course, it has not been practicable to give names of chorus members because we have enjoyed the company of so many, without whose excellence we would never have been required to perform.

Singing has given us a wide circle of friends, and one can guarantee that we meet some of them at any musical function we attend.

I am happy to record that grandson Luke plays 'cello, granddaughter Melissa saxophone, and grandson Jay guitar.

The following chapter deals with other aspects of our singing life.

Chapter 42 - Teaching

Our lack of involvement with choral societies from this time onwards did not herald the termination of other singing activities. The teaching of singing technique and interpretation has continued, Audrey since 1982 and I from 1984, including Adult Education classes at Hellesdon and Drayton (Audrey), I at Fakenham, and both of us at Wensum Lodge, Norwich (four classes) and Sharrington Village Hall. We opted out of Wensum Lodge classes after teaching there for seven years, but at the moment of writing, have continued to teach at Sharrington under the auspices of Sheringham Adult Education Centre.

In all our teaching, everyone has received individual tuition, and it would need considerable research to give a complete list of names of those whose technique and interpreting abilities we have endeavoured to improve or perfect. Undoubtedly such a list would be counted in hundreds.

The human voice will never cease to be the most beautiful of instruments when properly used, and, as teachers, we have endeavoured to direct pupils in the physiological and emotional aspects of singing, in order to attain the highest achievements of which their natural talents are capable.

We are extremely privileged in being allowed to attempt this, in the knowledge that one is asking of one's pupils the portrayal of every emotion of the mind, including pity, sorrow, hope, anger, happiness, love etc.

In our teaching work we have enjoyed tremendous assistance from pianists, who, apart from their expertise, artistic and sight-reading abilities, have had the patience to sustain the sometimes stop/go aspect of teaching. I hope I will not accidentally miss anyone out when I list the names of these pianists to whom we have been indebted over the years: Vaughan Brooks, Joyce Cannon, Gladys Holmes, Margaret Johnson, Celia Joyce, Grace Jude, Margaret Garner, Sylvia Ord, Cecily Grant, John Barnett, Michael Allard, Roger Bowen, Tony Ireland, Judith Evans, James Lilwall, Claire McArthur, Mark Riches, and Paul Winter. Deserving a special mention are Peter Cooper, Mary Tuffrey and Christian Stirling, who are presently still assisting us after many years of their invaluable support. Christian has been assisting me for nearly seven years and in spite of his many musical activities and accomplishments he has never failed to respond to the demands I have made upon his time. As I write this, he has, at the age of 27, just been appointed Director of Music at the Notre Dame High School, and together with two pupils, Anthea Eames and Josie Bramley, Audrey and I are about to open a bottle of bubbly to celebrate with him.

Peter Cooper and Mary Tuffrey, both excellent, are also still with us, and we are indebted to them for their forbearance and fortitude in sustaining, for so many occasions, the stop-go nature of our instruction.

Chapter 43 – 'Wings of Song'

To complete these memoirs, I must write about Audrey's 'Wings of Song' ladies choir.

Founded by her in 1990 and directed by her ever since, membership has risen from its original twelve to its present level of thirty (year 2001), as listed below.

Singers

Jean Allinson	Jillian Chadwick	Yvonne Ireson
Anne Aldis	Penny Cooke	Kathy Matsell
Catherine Ambler	Maureen Cope	Ann Moore
Renée Astley	Barbara Cozens	Brenda Plackett
Esmé Bagnall-Oakley	Anthea Eames	Dot Russ
Cathie Bailey	Margaret Gallant	Yvonne Scott
Josephine Beard	Jean George	June Smith
Marion Blake	June Harrison	Yvonne Symnick
Josephine Bramley	Veronica Haynes	Joan Thackery
Janet Bowen	Ann Hodgson	Rosemary Whittle

Accompanist	**Director**	**Page-turner**
Annette Jude	Audrey Yates	Mary Harris

The following is a list of their public performances to date.

Venue	Guest Artistes	& Accompanists
1990		
The Barbirolli Room		
Norwich Cathedral	Robert Yates	Margaret Garner
St Mary the Virgin Church,	Robert Yates	Margaret Garner
Wiveton		
Hethersett Old Hall School	Robert Yates	Margaret Garner
St Mary's Church, Old Hunstanton	Robert Yates	Vaughan Brookes
1991		
The Methodist Church, Hethersett	Robert Yates	Vaughan Brookes
St Edmund's Church, Old Costessey		
St Nicholas Church, Blakeney		
Prince's Street United Reformed		
Church, Norwich		
Wensum Lodge, Norwich	Robert Yates	Vaughan Brookes
Holy Trinity Church, Winterton	Richard White	Mark Bredin
St Mary's Church, Drayton		

1992

Reepham Parish Church	Robert Yates Rita Birchem
St Gregory's Church, Norwich	Norma Wick
Bawdeswell School	Glenn Bramley Vaughan Brookes
Assembly House, Norwich	Charles Roberts
St Andrew's Church, Buxton	Robert Yates Vaughan Brookes
St Mary's Church,	
North Tuddenham	Jeffrey Davies Cicely Grant
Maddermarket Theatre, Norwich	
St Edmund's Church, Old Costessey	

1993

St Mary's Church,	
North Tuddenham	
Assembly House, Norwich	Richard Woodburn – Trumpet
	Elizabeth Edwards – Flute
	Catherine Whitefield – Soprano
Reepham Parish Church	The Norwich Wind Ensemble
St Nicholas Church, Wells	Howard and Jan Eaton
St Margaret's Church, Cley	Robert Yates Vaughan Brookes
Castle Keep, Norwich	
St Gregory's Church, Norwich	Robert Yates Vaughan Brookes

1994

The Methodist Church, Hethersett	John Burdett – Oboe Anna Burdett
St Margaret's Church, Drayton	Zaharat Power-Clare
Whitlingham Hospital Conservatory	Norwich Citadel Brass Ensemble
St Paul's Church, Norwich	Norma Wick
Prince's Street United Reformed	
Church, Norwich	Neville Miller
St Andrew's Church, Hingham	Charles Roberts
	Robert Yates Vaughan Brookes
Bawdeswell Village Hall	Norma Wick
Blickling Hall	Glenn Bramley Mark Riches

1995

St Nicholas Church, Dereham	
St Andrew's Hall, Norwich	Christopher Payne – Trombone
	Norwich Citadel Band
	Robert Yates Vaughan Brookes
Trinity United Reformed	
Church, Norwich	
Blackfriars' Hall, Norwich	The Norwich Wind Ensemble
Bawdeswell Village Hall	Robert Yates Vaughan Brookes

1996

Wymondham Abbey	Gordon Pullin Vaughan Brookes
Trinity United Reformed Church, Norwich	
Norwich Cathedral	Drayton Band
St Mary's Church, North Tuddenham	Norma Wick
Blickling Hall	Robert Yates Vaughan Brookes

1997

Trinity Methodist Church, Dereham	
Cromer Parish Church	Brian Lincoln – Organ
	Robert Yates Vaughan Brookes
All Saints' Church, Bawdeswell	Charles Roberts
Hethersett Methodist Church	Tony Ireland
Prince's Street United Reformed Church, Norwich	Martin Plackett – Guitar

1998

Blickling Hall	Robert Yates Vaughan Brookes
Assembly House, Norwich	Glenn Bramley Christian Stirling
The Village Hall, Hoveton	Maggie Secker
St Nicholas Parish Church, North Walsham	David Fitzgerald – Saxophone
	Mark Bredin Christian Stirling
Claxton Opera Spring Concert Series	Richard White

1999

The Noverre Concert Room Assembly House, Norwich	The Amici Singers of Bedfordshire
Hethersett Methodist Church	
Blickling Hall	Gordon Pullin
	Samantha Muir – Guitar
	Christian Stirling – Piano
Barclay's Banking Hall, Norwich	Charles Roberts

2000

Assembly House, Norwich	Margery and Peter Cooper – Pianoforte duets
St Thomas Church, Norwich	James Lilwall – Organ
Cromer Parish Church	Matthews' Norfolk Brass Conducted by Christian Stirling

Yet to be performed as I write:

St Thomas' Church, Norwich   James Lilwall – Organ
St Peter and St Paul Church
   East Harling   James Lilwall – Organ
Noverre Suite, Assembly House,
   Norwich   Andrew Giller – Pianoforte
Wymondham Abbey   Wymondham Youth Orchestra

Photo: Peter King   **Wings of Song at Blickling**

Audrey owes a great debt of gratitude to Rita Birchem, who accompanied the choir from its inception in 1990 until the first concert of 1999 at the Assembly House. Her musicianship and dedication were of inestimable value to the founding and development of the choir. Additionally, she created and maintained a record of 'Wings of Song' performances in illustrative form, and in impeccable style.

Since then, Audrey has been extremely fortunate in securing the services and friendship of another excellent pianist, Annette Jude, and the continuity of 'Wings of Song' has thus been assured. There have been three occasions when Rita and Annette have not been available and Audrey has been fortunate enough to find deputies in Peter Cooper and Judy Tovey, both excellent, both friends.

Throughout 'Wings of Song' history, the intrepid, unflappable Mary Harris has acted as 'turner-over' for the pianist. The adjectives I have used are in the knowledge that the job is one calling for precise and calm action, anticipating the pianist's requirements.

Nothing can confirm the group's high standard of attainment so much as does a C.D. recording, which they made in the autumn of year 2000. This recording was made, over two days, by Roger Mayor of the Schools Recording Service, Chedgrave, at a studio in an adapted barn at Maypole Green, near Raveningham.

There is a little story to tell about my last performance at Blickling Hall. I should have been performing duets (Victorian and operatic) with Gordon Pullin, tenor. On the day of the concert, Gordon 'phoned, croaking. I was therefore obliged to sing three songs and three operatic arias instead of the declared programme. The only opportunity for rehearsal was in the Great Hall itself, sufficiently early to precede the arrival of audience. Happily, Vaughan and I had performed the pieces before, so we rehearsed more or less mezzo–voce. Unhappily, poor Vaughan couldn't speak, since he had developed an enormous cancer greatly impinging upon the lung, and I remain deeply indebted to him in his determination to see the job through in spite of his appalling physical problem. Happily, again, I am able to report that he had the thing removed (8 inches by 4 inches he advised) and, as I write, he is perfectly well.

As I have said in my previous chapter, Audrey and I have continued teaching and most of our activities in that capacity are directed to members of 'Wings of Song'. The word 'teaching' however is not quite accurate; 'coaching' is more apt, because all of Audrey's singers have had considerable tuition before and since 'Wings of Song' inception. In fact a large proportion of her choir members were recruited from adult education singing classes, where we have endeavoured to instil into pupils the elements of good singing and interpretation. So, in 'coaching' we aim at perfecting these elements. Solo performances are therefore encouraged; to which end we arrange recitals given to invited audiences. The standard of singing in 'Wings of Song' reflects, in my opinion, the dedication of its individual members in attaining the optimum quality and interpretative ability in the performance of this art.